D1622177

I Remember Rippey

A Collection of Remembrances

On the Occasion

Of Our 150th Anniversary

1870-2020

Made Possible by a Grant from

Greene County Community Foundation

To the Friends of Rippey

Published by Raspberry Ridge Publishing

Jefferson, Iowa

City of Rippey
P.O. Box 230
Rippey, Iowa
50235

Dan Brubaker, Mayor
Mary Millard, City Clerk

Greetings to Rippey community members, and those with roots in our town:

A birthday is a very special occasion and we are pleased to share with each of you our collected memories of Rippey so that you can join in our celebration. We hope that you will read and re-read these remembrances and enjoy reflecting and reminiscing about your own experiences and history.

As you know, we planned to celebrate the 150th birthday of the town on August 1, 2020, but because of the impact of coronavirus, we postponed the celebration until June 5, 2021. We look forward to seeing you then.

In actuality Rippey will be celebrating 166 years, since the original town was about 3 and ½ miles southwest. Old Rippey was established 16 years before the town was moved to access the railroad. New Rippey was planned in 1870.

The Friends of Rippey, the Sesquicentennial Committee, along with the City Council and I, have worked together nearly a year planning for the celebration, and those plans include a parade, an old timer's baseball game, a band concert, and fireworks.

Leading up to June 2021, you can observe the painting of a mural on the side of the Rolling Hills Bank, depicting a steam locomotive and other designs that are a part of own town's history. You will also see continued efforts to improve the Rippey Baseball Park, now known as Walt Anderson Field.

We anticipate completing the remodeling of the former Rippey school gymnasium into the fire station, allowing all the equipment to be stored in one location. An open house will show you how we have repurposed the school building to benefit the community.

In the neighborly spirit of our small town, Rippey welcomes you every day, but especially for this wonderful 150th birthday event. Read the remembrances, reflect on your own connections, and join us in celebration June 5, 2021.

Sincerely yours,

Dan Brubaker, Mayor

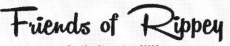 

Box 52 • Rippey, Iowa 50235

Dear Friends of Rippey, Rippey Alumni, and those who call Rippey their home:

We hope that you have enjoyed reading "I REMEMBER RIPPEY' stories on the Friends of Rippey (FOR) website and Facebook page. Thirty-three authors contributed and their stories were published electronically. Others shared brief thoughts and Facebook comments.

In 2020 Friends of Rippey received funding from the Greene County Community Foundation to print this booklet featuring Rippey memories. Even though the sesquicentennial had to be postponed until June of 2021, we are publishing the remembrances now for you to read and reflect upon with your families and friends.

While Rippey has physically diminished in population during the past years, the many of us who were fortunate to grow up in this nurturing, loving community remain influenced by our experiences and are proud to call Rippey home. Several persons wanted to aid financially for the upcoming celebration while honoring a deceased family member. We thank and honor those who have donated memorials. Please see listing.

Rippey 150th merchandise was provided at no cost to the Friends of Rippey by Clark Fessler, of T.C.& B. Corporate Wearables, and, of course, may be purchased and sent to you. The information about the sesquicentennial merchandise is on the front page of the Friends of Rippey website and in the back of the booklet.

Rippey High School Memorial bricks are available to anyone for $50, and the order form is available also on the website. Up to 4 lines may be inscribed on each brick. Please see the form in the back of the booklet.

When the Friends of Rippey was formed in 2001, we were led by Rippey leader and friend to all, Velda DeMoss, until her death in 2014. The not-for-profit organization was formed for "charitable, educational and scientific purposes" and has generated funds for various community projects including the electronic Rippey News, the Rippey Library, and the Rippey Community Room.

We are pleased to be aiding in the planning of the 150th birthday party, and look forward to continuing to remember Rippey in June of 2021.

Sincerely,

Mary Weaver

Mary Weaver,
President, Friends of Rippey

Friends of Rippey, a not for profit 501 c 3, created in 2001 to serve as catalyst for community enrichment

Hail to Rippey Fight Song

Tune: Minnesota Rouser

Hail to Rippey, Hats off to thee!

To our colors, true we will ever be.

Firm and strong, united are we,

Rah, rah, rah, rah-rah-rah!

Hail to thee Rippey High.

Photo Courtesy Merle Coon

Table of Contents

School Days

Sports Memories

Life on the Farm

Mining

Neighbors and Other Characters

Interviews

LaVere Derry

Mary Cunningham

Notes

LaVere Derry

An Interview with LaVere Derry

Rippey Community's Oldest Male Citizen in 2020

Interviewed by Mary Dorris Weaver

LaVere Derry was born at home on February 5, 1931, to his parents Vern and Lorene, with the assistance of a mid-wife, Minnie Morain. He was the firstborn of a brother and later a sister. He lived east of Rippey and went to school half days for kindergarten, and the mothers of his class took turns driving the children to school. In first grade when he went to school all day, he rode the bus. He attended the Rippey Consolidated School.

Growing up on a farm, he learned farm chores helping his father raise pigs and cattle. He gathered the eggs for his mom and said he was supposed to help in the garden, but was probably little help. He learned to milk a cow, though the milk was primarily for the family's use.

In 1948 LaVere had the Grand Champion Angus heifer at the Greene County Achievement show held in Scranton.

He was given the nick name *Cooke* while in high school and it has stuck with him for life. He graduated from the Rippey Consolidated High School in 1948 and entered the service during the Korean conflict, though was stationed in Germany for 18 months. Upon his return LaVere married Beverly Todd in 1954. From the union two children, Mike and Theresa (Teri), were born.

He purchased a car after he was married, and a motorcycle with a side car, for his new bride to travel with him.

When queried, LaVere said that he drove horses in the field, but never learned how to harness them.

He can recall when Claude States ran the funeral home west of the current Methodist Church at the former Lester

High home. Mr. States also ran the hardware store in Rippey.

When questioned about the best thing happening in his lifetime, LaVere thinks it may have been when water was pumped into the house and no longer had to be carried in, nor did the family have to use an outdoor toilet.

One of LaVere's fondest memories of Rippey is on Saturday evenings, when the high school band would climb onto the bandstand, and a concert would be held under the stars. The merchants were busy and people gathered to visit and share local stories.

We thank LaVere, aka *Cooke*, for sharing his stories and for his volunteer services to our community.

Mary Cunningham (Center), her Granddaughter
Jennifer Brant Eiteman

(Left), and Great Granddaughter Delany Eiteman
(Right)

An Interview with Mary Cunningham

Rippey Community's Oldest Female Citizen in 2020

Interviewed by Mary Dorris Weaver

Mary Ethel Cunningham, age 93, was born at home with the assistance of a mid-wife and Doc Martin. She was the only child of Leeta and Robert. Her parents moved to Rippey in 1928 and she lived near or as she describes, "under the water tower." She walked to school, starting in 1932 to the "new" Rippey Consolidated School, graduating in 1944 at 16 years of age. Her first job was substituting for the fifth-grade teacher who was absent due to a family illness. Her first paycheck earned her $3.00 per day substitute teaching as a new high school graduate.

She describes helping her Mom with the household chores of gardening, raising chickens, and canning as a child. She recalls at age 11, when Doctor Chase had to sew up her knee after she had a severe biking accident on the unmelted ice by the locker plant. (Formerly located between the Rebekah Hall and the beauty shop/yellow Hawkeye House). Her knee was ripped open through her snow pants and the cut was so deep the bone could be seen. She was held in place by her parents as Doc Chase repaired the wound, since he did not use any anesthesia or Novocain.

She can recall her Dad going to work at the coal mines around Rippey, including the Greene County Coal and McElheney mines. Her Dad also worked as a farm helper earning $1.00 per day, 6 days a week, providing his own lunch and transportation.

She describes the fun she and the other neighbor kids had when the water tower would occasionally overflow, and they could splash around in the water under the tower. She was a natural athlete and could play baseball with the Zanotti boys and one other girl. Her parents also had purchased a croquet set, and she enjoyed that game.

She worked in the telephone office, served as a bookkeeper, and assisted in households prior to becoming the bride of Kenneth Cunningham in 1947. Her mother had taught her to can, and she had a goal of 100 quarts of tomatoes and 50 quarts of beans every season.

When queried she said she only had one professional permanent for her hair. She learned to cut her own hair, as well as provide home permanents for her family members.

The biggest and best change that happened to Rippey in her memory was the paving of every street in the town.

In a follow-up phone call, Mary subsequently thought the biggest change could have been the tiling of the area of the Rippey baseball field. Prior to the county tile being put in place, the field would flood going across the now County Road, P-46, up to the Methodist Church parking lot. She was told part of a jingle... "Ben Osborn and ole Saul J. (Johnson) went for a boat ride on Ridles' Bay." (Ridles were the owners of the property originally).

She recalled a shuffleboard located in a park near the former water tower, now the Rippey Fire Station. She and the city kids would play hours of shuffleboard. She said the flooring could be picked up in case of flooding,but was probably 8 feet wide by 20 feet long.

She has many wonderful stories, and reported the park, known as Osborn Park, was originally called the Soldier's Park, and trees were planted there in recognition of the many soldiers who had served in WWI.

She said she and her husband Ken, who drove the Standard Oil Tank Wagon, were entertained by going to the movies in Perry, or to dances. They also played bridge and pinochle with friends in the community.

Her children, David and Kathy, were born at the Greene County Hospital in Jefferson, with Dr. Chase in attendance.

She resides south of Rippey with her family and is pictured here with her granddaughter, and her great grandchild. She remains mentally sharp, is well informed regarding current affairs, and has strong political beliefs that she willingly shares.

We thank her for her contributions to our remembrances.

* Michelle Fields, drainage coordinator for Greene County replied: "The tiles that drain the west side of town to the east belong to Drainage District 119. My records show landowners petitioned the Greene County Board of Supervisors to create that district in March of 1916 and that construction was completed in July of 1917."

Notes

Early History of Rippey

An Element of the Mural Painted in Rippey, Iowa
By Sarah Stotts   Summer 2020

Some Early Settlers of the Rippey Area
By Roger L. Crumley MD   May 10, 2020

Doing some family genealogy while being self-quarantined for coronavirus mitigation, I discovered some interesting facts about the earliest days of Greene County, Iowa. Greene County was created out of Dallas County in the 1850's. While Truman Davis was the first settler of the new County, at least one account has it that Sylvanus G. Crumley was the second (1850). Both lived near the Raccoon ("Coon") River between the subsequent sites of Jefferson and Old Rippey. *(Another account has Enos Buttrick and Richard Hardin, to have arrived next after Davis.) (Buttrick's creek, Hardin creek)*

Sylvanus Crumley's father was Rev. Isaac D. Crumley, whose wife Rachel had died in Virginia earlier that same year (1850). It is not known if Rev. Isaac had decided to make the move to Iowa because the Methodist Church asked him to, whether he felt adventurous (he was 53 years old in 1850), or possibly just wanting to re-start his life after his wife died.

In any event, Rev. Isaac Crumley decided to move to the frontier land's Greene County, IA. He came to Iowa via a "prairie schooner" (covered wagon) drawn by 5 oxen (or horses). His travelling group also included his son Sylvanus, his first son William P. Crumley, his 2 married daughters, Lydia and Hannah Crumley, and their 2 husbands (Babb) who were brothers. Another son (Isaac D. Crumley, Jr) arrived at the same time, or shortly thereafter. Lydia Crumley was married to Valentine S. Babb, and Hannah Crumley's husband was Kelley S. Babb. One of the Babb couples also had a baby who apparently made and survived the arduous trip. Imagine the rigors of that 850-mile trip by covered wagon from Virginia to

Greene County, Iowa with very few bridges and only a few roads, at least for the last 400 miles. They found that their new area had only 1 or 2 other "white" settlers, while Indians, wigwams, elk, and deer were abundant. (*Rev. Isaac Crumley was my great, great grandfather, and his son William P. Crumley my great grandfather.*)

The group stopped for a few days in the area of current Dallas County, ostensibly for supplies, and then moved on to Greene County. The 2 Babb families, and 3 Crumley boys/young men began to settle in the area near the Coon River, southeast of Jefferson, and thought to be near (if not actually in) the site of what was to become Old Rippey. Having arrived in 1850, these early settlers were there before either Jefferson or Rippey were surveyed and platted (Jefferson, 1854; Rippey (1855).

The subsequent surveyors/planners of Jefferson were George S. Walton and Robert M. Rippey, and surveyors/planners of Old Rippey were Judge Norman S. Daniels and William P. Crumley, with survey signed by Robert M. Rippey.

But times were hard, winters severe, and no amenities were nearby. The nearest post office was 50 miles away at Fort Des Moines, and they had to travel to Warren, Marion and Mahaska counties for provisions and supplies, with no roads to mark their course or bridges to cross the many creeks and rivers.

Deer and elk were plentiful, but only until the winter of 1855-56. That year the snow was so heavy that these deer and elk could not escape various predators, many of which included the settlers with clubs. It is said that ever since that winter the Greene County area has had relatively few deer and elk.

The County began organizing in 1854. The first officers were William Phillips, county judge; Sylvanus G. Crumley, county clerk; Treasurer and Recorder, James H. Phillips; Sheriff, Rev. Isaac D. Crumley; County Attorney, Norman S. Daniels. So interestingly Greene County's first Sheriff was a Methodist minister (Isaac D. Crumley, Sr.)

In any event, the Crumleys were active in the new county order. Not long thereafter came the Civil War. Isaac D. Crumley, Jr. was killed in the war, and William P. Crumley (my great grandfather), also fighting with the Union Army, came home to Old Rippey on furlough from the Civil War in April, 1861. He got sick and died of "black measles" (prob. either smallpox or Rocky Mountain Spotted Fever) at his home in Old Rippey on April 15, 1861. He was only 37 years old. His son William Halsey Crumley (my grandfather) was born 3 days later. Wm. Halsey operated mercantile/grocery stores in Rippey until he died in May 1935.

George S. Walton and Sylvanus G. Crumley jointly operated the Walton and Crumley General Store in Jefferson. Rev. Isaac Crumley lived to the ripe old age of 90 (died in 1887), as did his daughter Hannah, who died in 1918 after subsequently moving to Jefferson. (Hannah H. Smith.) So Rev. Isaac Crumley and his 5 offspring arrived in Greene County together in May 1850, and many subsequent Crumleys remained in the Rippey/Jefferson area for many generations thereafter.

Carte-de-visite portrait of Captain Robert Montgomery Rippey who served in the Civil War with Company E of the 39th Iowa Volunteer Infantry. ca1862. Photo capture from album.

Photocopy provided by Laura Cummings Miller Collection, Special Collections, State Historical Society of Iowa, Des Moines. Contributed by Lynn Wilson.

How Our Town Got Its Name
By Lynn Wilson

I was born and raised in Rippey, and probably like most people, I didn't give much thought when I was growing up about how our town got its name. When I attended the 1970 Centennial, I looked at the excellent History of Rippey, and Families of Rippey publications, and learned that our town was named for a Civil War Captain, Robert M. Rippey. Much later, when I decided to do genealogy on the Wilson family, which I quickly traced back to England (my great grandparents), I enjoyed the project so much that I decided to do some research on Captain Rippey.

Following is a summary of what I found, after researching the Greene County Records, Iowa Historical Society, Indiana Historical Records, Elkhart, Indiana County Records, and the Vicksburg, Corinth, and Shiloh National Battlefields. I also received much help from the Jefferson, Iowa, Public Library.

Robert Montgomery Rippey was born in Rush County, Indiana, on August 17, 1828, one of five children of Mathew and Jane Montgomery Rippey. During his early years, his parents moved to the Elkhart, Indiana, area, where Robert grew up. His parents were very prominent farmers, with substantial land holdings. They were active supporters of the community, engaging in a number of philanthropic causes. Mathew was also a Justice of the Peace and a state representative. Robert attended DePauw University in Greencastle, Indiana, in 1850 for one year. During the early 1850's Robert moved to Greene County, Iowa, becoming one of its earliest, most prominent and influential citizens, serving as a drainage commissioner, surveyor, and County Judge. On page 188 in the History of Rippey, published in 1970, just before the Centennial, is a plat of the original town, called Old Rippey, surveyed by Robert M. Rippey in 1855. The town was then named for him.

On February 14, 1856, Robert married Ann Linn. One daughter, Olive Jane, was born. After the death of Ann, Robert married Mary E. Young on July 22, 1857. One daughter, Alice Ann, was born.

When the Civil War began, Mr. Rippey answered the call of duty, and was commissioned as a Captain in Company E, 39th Iowa Volunteer Infantry Regiment, on August 24, 1862. Ten companies were formed, with a total of 933 men, commanded by Colonel Cummings and Lt. Colonel Redfield. The 39th was transported by rail to Cairo, Illinois, and then sailed down the Mississippi River to Columbus, Kentucky, seeing their first action at Parker's Crossroads, Tennessee, in December 1862. The regiment spent most of 1863 guarding important Union installations in Corinth, Mississippi. In 1864 the regiment moved south, engaging in a number of battles, including participating in General Sherman's march to the sea through Georgia. The regiment sustained heavy losses and received the highest commendation for bravery from General Sherman. The regiment capped its distinguished career by participating, after the war ended, in the Grand March in Washington, D.C., on May 24, 1865. The 39th was formally mustered out of service at Clinton, Iowa, on June 06, 1865. According to the official records, the 39th Iowa Volunteer Infantry lost, due to disease and combat, 192 enlisted men, and 8 officers, for a total of 200.

Captain Rippey died at Corinth, Mississippi, on October 30, 1863, of acute dysentery, age 35. He is buried along with his first wife and two daughters in the Jefferson, Iowa, Cemetery.

The burial site is on the east side of the drive, just south of the entry to the cemetery

Old Rippey Moves to the Railroad
By Mary Dorris Weaver

Newspaper quote provided by Jean Darling Borgeson
The original Rippey began in 1855 when the Davis, Hardin, and Buttrick families and several others arrived and formed a neighborhood cluster of early pioneers along the North Raccoon River in southeastern Greene County.

The stagecoach from Des Moines to Fort Dodge, and eventually to Sioux City, ran through the town, as the trail essentially followed the Raccoon River across Greene County from southeast to northwest. The stagecoach ran through original Rippey from 1850-1866.

New Rippey was laid out in 1870 by William Cartwright as an employee of the Des Moines Valley Railroad.

The first homes in Rippey were moved from Coal Town, later called Angus, and Surrey. Both were coal mining communities that were abandoned as the coal supply diminished. Surrey, or Surry as it is sometimes spelled, is no longer visible, but was located three and one half miles south of Rippey, and one half mile east.

Jefferson Bee, Friday, April 28, 1871; pg. 3 Al Swaim, Editor & Proprietor:

Rippey Station—The manner in which New Rippey has been taken with the fever of improvement of late is gratifying, and that we shall soon have a fair-sized community of industrious people gathered together there, promises most details. The improvements are marks that bring gratification to everyone who desires the thousands of untilled acres to bloom and blossom as the gardens of the storied past. Our domain is wide, healthy and fruitful, and that its advantages are being well canvassed and fell in with, we have only to point to the numberless farms now being open and to the white covered wagons and tents dotting the green prairie in almost every part of the county.

Mr. Cartwright was an investor who resided in Mediapolis, Iowa, and had purchased about 40 acres of land on either side of the railroad in and around Rippey. The railroad was called the Des Moines Valley Railroad, later to become the Des Moines and Fort Dodge and eventually the Minneapolis/St Louis. (M and St. L.).

Passenger services, from all research of older newspapers, began in May of 1869. We have documentation the passenger train carried soldiers to the Spanish American War, but the permanent depot was not built until 1872. It was built of wood and painted red and sat on the east side of the railroad tracks, just north of Main Street. It had three rooms, a waiting room, a telegraph office and a freight room. There were outside pens for livestock south of the depot. The only interior furnishings were the heavy wooden slatted seats with iron legs and arm rests. These seats were arranged around the outside of the room, which was heated by a pot-bellied stove that burned coal and stood in a shallow wooden box which was partly filled with ashes. This served to catch any embers which might fall from the stove door. The room was lighted by oil-filled lamps on side brackets.

The railroad did a thriving business with passengers and car-load shipments of grain, livestock, and coal.

Passenger service reached its peak in 1912 when there were four passenger trains each way daily, which included a night train with a sleeping car.

In the paper issued on Thursday July 9, 1925, "Rippey News" shows this passenger rail schedule:

North Bound	No. 209	1:50 P.M.
	No. 205	6:59 P.M.
South Bound	No. 206	4:59 P.M.
	No. 210	8:48 A.M.

An ad was also in the newspaper encouraging the purchase of tickets for the Iowa State Fair and to ride the train to the Fair.

Part of the mystique of visiting the depot was watching and listening to the telegraph. Its primary use was for sending train orders, but before the telephone it was the only way important messages could be shared. Every agent had to master the Morse Code. The election returns came by telegram to the depot and huge crowds would gather on election night, eager to learn the outcome.

The last passenger service was April 1959.

The depot was torn down and the lumber burned in 1963.

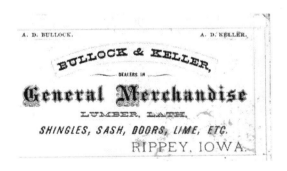

Notes

The Town

Radebaugh and Munson Grain Office and Elevator circa 1900

Churches Circa 1890

Country Doctor
By David Chase

Walter E. Chase (my Dad) was the doctor in Rippey for 33 years. Born and raised in St. Louis, he worked his way through pre-med and medical school at Washington University there. He then interned at Iowa Methodist Hospital in Des Moines where he met Elsie Pearl Henry (my Mom). She was just finishing nurse's training. They married on July 31, 1933, and immediately headed to Rippey which was at the time advertising for a doctor. Dad was that guy and Mom was his nurse. Despite having very little money, in the fall they opened an office in a small white frame building just south of Killam's Hardware Store. It rented for $15 a month and had been vacant for some time, so there was some fixing up to do. It had a small entrance/waiting area, a drug room and a treatment room. Soundproof? Hardly! They kept a radio on in the waiting area to shelter from curious ears the patient/doctor consultations going on in the next room. Office hours were from 9 to noon and 2 to 5 on weekdays and 7 am to 9 pm on Saturdays. House calls (yes, house calls!) were made before 9 and after 5 except for emergencies which were tended to any time. They kept the drug room stocked and their charge was only for the cost of drugs dispensed. Doc also fit glasses. After 10 years of practice, they increased their office call charge to $2 a visit plus drugs. House calls were $3 plus drugs.

The Greene County Hospital was opened in 1939 and Doc was on its first medical staff. He saw patients both there and at the Dallas County Hospital in Perry. Rounds at either or both were made either before or after office hours. Prior to the opening of the hospitals, babies were delivered at home. Many a bed or kitchen counter were made into makeshift delivery tables. They made their trips to these delivery sites in a 1930 Model A Ford battling mud, snow and an occasional blizzard. On some occasions, farmers had to come and get Doc and Pearl in a bobsled!

In between their busy/stressful lives of a country doctor and nurse my folks managed to have three children, Dolores, Paul and myself. Doc delivered all three of us. We were the true benefactors of the quality of life in Rippey, even the trials and tribulations of being a country doctor's kids. Many an evening meal was interrupted by a knock at the door or an emergency call. I recall farmers arriving at the front door with injuries from their work, many times with fingers, hands, arms, etc. dangling due to a run-in with a grain auger or a disgruntled sow. Without exception, it was "Doc, patch me up; I have to get back to the field!" Which he did. (Mom, pass the green beans!)

Doc found time to become first President of the Rippey Lions Club and Pearl was choir director at the Methodist Church for many years. They loved to travel and that wanderlust was passed on to their children. Stress release for Doc was on the golf course where his mild-mannered demeanor sometimes gave way to an "Incredible Hulk" persona, especially if he missed a two-foot putt! But he never carried that back to his practice or his beloved patients. He could be described as a Master of bedside manner and the soft touch.

Doc and Pearl "retired" from country practice in 1966 when Doc accepted the Director of Student Health position at the University of Northern Iowa. They retired to Sun City, Arizona, in 1973. Pearl died in 1986 and Doc died in 2000. Both are buried in the Rippey Cemetery under a headstone that declares: "Served Rippey for 33 Years". They loved their time here and all of their wonderful patients who were also their friends. Accordingly, this is where they wanted to finally rest

Rippey Fire Department

Jointly submitted by Mary Weaver, Jean Borgeson and Peter Johnson

(Excepts from full article available on Rippey Library site)

Rippey had its first organized volunteer fire department in 1911 with 24 men on the fire team. The city water works was installed in 1911, and the volunteers were subsequently organized. (*History of Rippey 1849-1956*).

Before 1911, during a fire, water was carried from the city well, or other nearby wells, via a bucket brigade. Men and women of all ages participated. Water soaked blankets and carpets were placed on adjoining roofs to minimize the sparks from the flames. Seldom was a major fire extinguished.

A later improvement was a small platform mounted on wheels about one foot high on which was a double action pump with two handles that were operated by two men. To this pump was attached a long hose with a nozzle. There was room on the platform for a large wash tub, where the end brigade recipient would pour the water into the tub, and it was pumped on the fire.

In a cupola atop the first firemen's headquarters was a large bell to which was attached a rope, so the first person arriving at the building could give the alarm by ringing the bell. After electricity came to the town, the fire siren was moved in 1915 to the adjoining building, the Crumley and States store. The telephone operators were given the responsibility of setting off the alarm for a fire, and also for time signals throughout the day, 7:00 a.m., 12:00 noon, and 6:00 p.m.

The current fire hall was built in 1994, at the location of the former water tower. It is a metal shed that allows the housing of the fire equipment. The rescue squad vehicle, the attack vehicle, the pumper and the tubes for grain bin rescue are stored in the building.

The current volunteer Fire Chief is Peter Johnson. There are fewer than 10 firefighters serving the town and township. The most recent fire truck was purchased in 2016 for $92,000, a gift from the estate of Bill Wisecup. The Friends of Rippey and the Washington Township Trustees aid in maintaining fire extinguishing and rescue equipment. Chief Johnson is a certified emergency medical responder. The Friends of Rippey have helped to secure grain rescue equipment, OSHA approved helmets, and radios to aid the Rippey Volunteer Firefighters. The Washington Township Trustees are Chairperson Mary Hick, Roger Norgren, and Tod Contner. Jean Borgeson is the township clerk.

Information was gathered from the Jefferson Bee, History of Rippey 1849-1970; and History of Rippey, 1849-1956.

Rippey Fire Dept. 1912

After the town water system was installed in 1919, a fire team was organized consisting of 24 men. They are identified as John Shoemaker, Arch Morse, Burley Meyers, Halsey Crumley, EA Shaw, Walter Roberts, John Haberer, Elijah Wade, Wayne Osborn, Lester Johnson, Ira White, James Chambers, John Dugan, Andrew Jensen, William Radebaugh, Claude Johnson, William Chambers, Jay States, IJ Burk, Sr., Arthur Frizelle, Lester Crumley, Claude States, Walter Dugan, NP Burk

A Recollection of Rippey in 1931
By Clark Bardole, 1981

A recollection of Rippey as it was 50 years ago when Clark started to work at the *First National Bank*, Rippey, in Sept. 1931. Compiled by Clark Bardole in 1981.

Business places starting at the East End of Main Street on the North Side of the street.

Starting East of railroad tracks.
Kirgis Implements and Corn Shelling
Gilliland & Riley (Stock Buyers)
Stock Yards and Depot

West of Tracks
Hotel Operated by Ella Brown Feith. Afterwards used as Movie House operated by A.V. Lauver and after that cream and egg buying station owned and operated by Alex Towers

Ferguson & Riley Café. B.M. Riley and Roy Ferguson, owners and operators

Grocery & Dry Goods Store Operated by Allen Senter & Son. Afterwards a hardware store operated by Claude States. Claude States was also a mortician and had funerals at his home in the house now occupied by Miriam High. Most funerals were held at the churches at that time.

Grocery and Dry Goods Operated by Mack and Lulu Davis.

First National Bank, Rippey, Iowa J.H. Van Scoy, Cashier; B.M. Riley, President;
Clark Bardole and Dorothea Dugan, Bookkeepers. In 1981, Max Riley has been the President continuously for 50 years.

Barbershop in Basement of Bank Ira Martin, Operator.

Post Office-North End of Bank George Fry, Post Master and Halsey Munson, Assistant Post Master; John Dugan and Russell Radebaugh, rural mail carriers.

West of the Bank and also west of Dr. Shipley's office there still were hitching posts to tie horses to while shopping. North from Post Office was City Fire Hall and in front of it was a watering trough for horses.

Grocery Store and Dry Goods owned and operated by Sarah Pelly and her brother. Across the street west of the First National Bank. Crumley and States formerly operated this store, Halsey Crumley and C.D. States. North of store was a cave for potatoes and other vegetables and Ice House with a barber shop in the basement of store where LeRoy Overman is in 1981.

Cream Station west of store and at one time a hamburger shop operated by Margaret Peterson Franklin

Restaurant operated by Harry McDowell

Rippey Savings Bank: Dwight Crumley, cashier, Theo Holmes, President,
Hugo Norgren and Margaret Moore (Burrell), Assistants

Between *McDowell Restaurant and Cream Station* in the summertime they had outside picture shows. Silent, of course.

Rippey Mutual Telephone Office Roy Blakely, lineman, and his wife Mrs. Blakely,phone operator

Fry Auto Company Everett Fry (Jigs) and his father, owners and operators. West from here at one time Thornton had harness and shoe shop and later Floyd Derry had a grocery store.

On Corner Dr. Shipley office and at one time Dr. Hubbard had dentist shop in basement.

Across the street West was Harvey Van Horn dwelling and filling station.
Glenn States operated the tank wagon.

Starting at East End of Main Street on the South side of the street across tracks
Standard Tanks and Rippey Oil company Harvey VanHorn owner and Jas McCormick was the Standard Oil man.

West side of tracks on Main Street; South side of street
Livery Barn Ira White, Chet Riley and Lewis Thornburgh previous owners and operators. I believe Lewis Thornburgh was the last operator. The owner of the livery barn also ran a dray service for deliveries arriving at depot for business houses.

Meat Market: W.E. Tuttle, owner and operator. Sankey John did butchering for meat markets and also went from farm to farm and did butchering for farmers and as I remember the price was $1.00 per animal.
NW Bell Telephone Company-operated by Hattie Smith King and Frances Bilson Garren. Same building used later for shoe shop.

Osborn Flats, east of corner drugstore above Osborn Drugstore, Cream and Egg station, millinery shop-Apartments

B.F. Osborn Drugstore: B.F. Osborn started in Rippey in 1878 and operated a drug store until his death about 1933. Building now vacant.

South from Drug Store *Dr. W.G. Martin, M.D. office.* Later *Dr. W.E. Chase office*
Across the street West from Drug Store was *Burk's Garage*-operated by Frank Burk.
Town Pump on Burk's corner.

I.O.O.F. Lodge-in basement *harness and shoe shop*, M. Adams operator.
South end of basement used for storage by Burk Auto Company.

Building West of I.O.O.F. Hall now used as Beauty Parlor by Eloise Overman. Previously used as Cream and Egg Station and feed store and Millinery shop.
I believe George Crandall operated the Cream Station at that time.

Dr. Rail was a veterinarian. *George Naylor,* Plumber, Knute Van Horn worked with wells. H.E. Smith ran dairy and did painting. S.D. McDowell was a painter. Burk and Harold McCain operated *Farm Dairy*. Harold McClain was also City Assessor.

Carpenters: Art Frizelle, George Mercer and Frank Glidden, John Porter (also known as Aaron) repaired watches.

Town Marshal part of the time Doug Garren and part of the time Everett John. Doug Garren was a brick mason also.

Everett John also did day work and sexton at cemetery. At that time (1931) digging a grave cost $10.00.

Tile ditchers: Everett John, Jesse Ervin, Ed Moore and Phil Miller.

John Dugan was auctioneer in addition to work as mail carrier.

Rippey formerly had its own newspaper but at that time same arrangement as we have now.

O.R. Stevens was just beginning his career as auctioneer and afterwards sale barn owner and operator.

Starting at Elevator on Percival Street across the tracks

Percival Street is first street north of Main St.

Clark Brown Grain Company John Munson, manager

West Side of tracks on Percival Street

E.J. Clapp-Blacksmith shop and horse shoeing. Jack Naylor also had a gas pump and lived in same building, just east of Blacksmith shop, on north side.

N.P. Burk & Co. On south side of street. Owned and operated by N.P. Burk and
his son, Oscar, operated a lumberyard.

On north side of street at 2nd and Percival: *F.R. Howard filling station and farm implements.* Then on 1st and Percival (where Maxine Johnson lived) was an *implement storage for F.R. Howard.* Top floor was *Masons' Lodge* and the building that was formerly a *Presbyterian church.*

West on Percival Street is the *Rippey Consolidated School as it was in 1931.*

Bijo Nichols had a *blacksmith shop* in the south part of town near the water tower.

Other information in 1931:
Rippey had a semi-pro baseball team. Three active churches, Methodist, Baptist and Christian. All located on the "Church" corners where the Methodist Church now stands. Lodges in Rippey were Masons, Eastern Star, I.O.O.F., Rebekah, Modern Woodmen and Royal Neighbors.

Louis Anschutz (grandfather of Donald Anschutz) was section boss.

Robert Groves (Bob) and Billy Johns both operated corn shellers and lived in the country.

In 1931, there were at least 35 different business places. Lots of business and social activities in the old town. In the summertime on Saturday nights, we had a free band concert in public square on a band wagon. On Wednesday nights outside picture shows shown against the brick wall of what was later Thornburgh's Café.

With Harry Cofer, Doug Garren and the Kinkead brothers, we had continuous entertainment with stories (some good and some bad). Before one was finished, another one was ready to be recited.

The changes in the farming community and modes of farming likewise changed tremendously. Fifty years ago, I would say at least 95% of the farmers had chickens, milk cows and hogs. In fact, the egg and cream checks were what kept most farmers in groceries and provided for other household expenses. At that time folks had very little but seemed to get along on what they had. With horses for farming and raising their own hay and grain to feed the horses, they didn't have nearly the farm expenses they do now. In spite of modern households and modern farm equipment and electricity, I would say people were just as happy and content as they are now (1981) and who knows, maybe more so.

If I have missed any business places in Rippey at that time (1931), it was not intentional.
Clark Bardole, Rippey, Iowa

Rippey Centennial Medal 1970

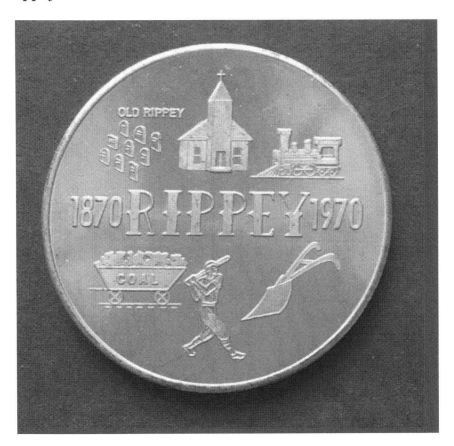

Rippey, Iowa, Main Street Businesses, 1950's

By Carol Norgren John with assistance from Nancy Bardole Hanaman, Mary Weaver, Phyllis McElheney Lepke

After reviewing a list of 1931 Main Street businesses provided by Nancy and Dale Hanaman, Carol Norgren John, with help from Nancy Bardole Hanaman, Mary Weaver, and Phyllis Lepke, put together this listing of Rippey businesses in the 1950s. This is not a definitive listing.

North side of Main Street from east to west:

Brobst Café   States Sundries   Empty building   First National Bank, on the corner

Around the corner to the north:

Post Office   Fire Station   Lumberyard

Saiter's grocery store on the corner with Shorty Overman barber shop in the basement and Masonic Lodge upstairs

Library, small building   Squeak Thornburg café   Rippey Savings Bank

Apartment building   Fry Auto Company   Nellie Senter grocery store

Telephone office

South side of Main Street from west to east:

(house) Eloise Overman beauty shop   Locker   Rebekah Hall   Burk Ford

Dr. Chase's office down the street   Killam Hardware
Legion Hall

Across the diagonal highway (144):

Co-op   Ross Hatfield gas station   Train station

The Library
By Mary Fry Liebich
The library was in a small wooden building between Thornburg's café and the grocery store. During the summer, there were movies that were shown on a screen between the cafe and library—the audience faced north and sat in lawn chairs they brought or on a blanket on the ground. We'd bring our own popcorn and pop.

Band Concerts
By Mary Dorris Weaver
I remember the Rippey band concerts on Main Street, then in the bandshell. Music under the Stars in Rippey.

McDowell's Phillips 66
By John Rains
I remember when McDowell's Phillips 66 was a place to hang out. I did learn a lot about cars hanging out there. Gas prices during the early Sixties averaged 33 cents per gallon!

Fun at the Cafe
By Jerald Fessler through his son, Clark Fessler

During the time that we played cards daily at Roy Brobst's Café, we would play right up until noon, go home for dinner, then go right back.

When GTE took over the telephone system in Rippey, they installed a phone booth on the sidewalk by the Legion Hall. While the man was installing the phone, "Dud" Kelleher was hanging over his shoulder watching. Franklin Johnson walked over from Roy's restaurant to read the number on the phone. He returned to the restaurant and dialed the number while the rest of us watched from the front window. Dud couldn't resist when the phone rang. Franklin pretended he was calling another person in another town and Dud was trying to tell him he was talking to Rippey, Iowa. After talking for some time, Franklin asked Dud if he would blow into the phone. We saw his cheeks swell, at which time Dud realized he had been pranked and hung up.

Breakfast at the Diner
By Jim F Johnston
I never lived in Rippey, but my grandfather used to go to breakfast at the diner where other friends and farmers would gather in the mornings and tell stories. He would take me along when I was visiting. Now when I see the "Liar's Table" at my local diner, I think of those breakfasts.

I Remember Rippey
By Lester Zanotti

Excerpts used with permission of Lester Zanotti, when he gave these remarks at the 60th anniversary of the class of 1954 at the Rippey Alumni Banquet in 2014.

Those of us who grew up in Rippey during the 40's and 50's really got Rippey at her best. People took pride in living here. There weren't any fancy beautiful homes, but what people had, they kept up—houses painted, lawns mowed, and there was no junk lying around. This was their town!!

And how about downtown? At one time, we had three grocery stores, Senter, Thornburgh, and Ed Galivan. Also two car dealerships. Jiggs Fry Chevrolet, and I.J.Burk, Ford. Two banks managed by Dwight Crumley and Clark Bardole. Thornburgh café, Library—LeRoy Overman barbershop and his wife, Eloise had a beauty salon across the street. We had a lumberyard. Jay States had the drugstore. You can see I am working my way down Main Street. Across the street was Killam's Hardware. Irwin Correy had the tavern until he was injured. We had a shoe repair shop run by a guy named Beanie. Back across the street, we had a pool hall run by Wes Rittgers. Down across the highway Leck High had a Mobile Station. Then, up the road Errol Wilson had the Phillips station. We were blessed to have Dr. Chase. Orrie Stevens had a great Sales Barn operation, which burned down, but afterwards he had one of the largest farm machinery sales businesses in the Midwest.

By today's standards, most of us were living in poverty conditions. No one complained because everyone was in the same boat. If you were fortunate enough to have a basement, you could have a coal stoker, which would heat your home around the clock and also give you hot water.

The rest of us had a coal or wood burning stove for cooking and warmth and a cold-water faucet. NO other inside plumbing. It wasn't that people couldn't afford anything else; it was just nothing else was available.

It wasn't until the late 40's when natural gas came to Rippey. I can remember when we got a gas stove for heat and indoor plumbing with a flush stool and hot water! Talk about home improvements.

Our Class Motto was, "Build for character, not for fame". None of my class became famous, but on the character issue, I believe that all of us who experienced growing up here had a very good foundation on which to build for who we are today.

Full Service Town
By John Rains

I remember when Rippey was a full service town—Grocery store, telephone company, barber shop, beauty shop, locker, two car dealerships, two banks, lumber yard, hardware store, two gas stations, two restaurants, pool hall, post office, grain elevator, two churches, school (kindergarten thru 12th), library. (Hopefully, I mentioned all.)

The Case Of The Inept Bank Robbers 1967
By Myron Rinker and Nancy Bardole Hanaman
with information written by Clark Bardole

In 1967, Clark Bardole wrote "We arrived for work and discovered that someone had entered the bank with the intention of entering the vault and safe." The would-be robbers had knocked off the knob that controlled the combination on the heavy safe door. The robbers were unable to enter the safe and nothing was stolen.

Before entering the bank, Myron Rinker recalled that the robbers cut the wires into the bank. They had entered the building from the basement area under the bank where there had been a barbershop at one time, Bette Wilcox' beauty salon, and a location for a group of card players, including Max Riley. The place of entry would indicate that the inept robbers knew the layout of the building and broke into the door at ground level and then the locked door at the top of the stairs into the bank. Clark Bardole wrote "Evidently the would-be thieves were amateurs."

The FBI was called since at the time this bank was chartered by the Federal government and an agent came from Des Moines. Larry Burkett, town marshal, was contacted and probably the county sheriff also. The locksmith came from Des Moines and worked half a day before the safe could be opened and repaired.

As the safe could not be opened at the beginning of regular banking hours, this presented a problem since there was no cash available. Clark also wrote "In order to get money to operate on that day, we got some from our friendly competitor, the Rippey Savings Bank." A wonderful example of small town care and cooperation.

Hold Up at People's Bank in Rippey, Oct. 2009

By Nancy Bardole Hanaman interviewing Myron Rinker
(Additional information from Jefferson newspapers)

A pleasant Saturday morning, October 17, 2009, at People's Bank in Rippey developed into a harrowing experience for Myron Rinker, Ashley Brelsford and Mel Jennings. Around 10 a.m., Myron saw a man walk across the street to the bank. As the man entered, he pulled out a gun and ordered Myron, Ashley, and Mel to lie on the floor. He demanded money from the employees who had been behind the counter and then entered the offices to ransack the women's purses and grab a set of car keys. He escaped in one of the employee's cars and traveled to the Rippey Cemetery where he had left another car. As soon as the robber exited, they locked the doors to the bank and called the Greene County Sheriff.

The harrowing experience continued at a later time when Myron and the bank employees were accompanied by the sheriff to the Federal Courthouse in Des Moines and testified at the trial of Jason Lee Bowles. Also in the Jefferson Herald was information that Bowles had committed robberies in Slater and St. Charles prior to the event in Rippey on October 17. Early the next week, he continued his crime spree at the First Trust and Savings Bank in Oxford. Following the Federal court case, he was convicted of the robberies in 2010.

Myron and the bank employees will always remember fearing for their lives at the scene of the robbery and their experiences following that day. Myron also recalled the helpful response of the county sheriff and others following the robbery at People's Bank in 2009.

School Days

1908

1913

1959

All Aboard! Trip from Rippey To Grand Junction In 1953
By Nancy Bardole Hanaman

Miss Maxine Johnson and Miss Evelyn Wilson gathered the excited, chattering students in Kindergarten and First Grade for the short trip to the Rippey Depot. They were embarking on a field trip to Grand Junction in the spring of 1953. For most of the children this was their first train ride and they were impatient and ready to go.

Among the eager students were Carol Norgren, Phyllis McElheney, Donald Bardole, Stephen Young, Joyce Bauer, Janis McElheney, Kindergarten; Judy McElheney, Susan Culley, Fred Grow, Marna Rittgers, Dennis Nelson, Dale Robson, Bob Scharingson, Janis Kenan, Jim Odin, Janice Woods, Nancy Bardole, First Grade.

We soon departed from our train journey at the depot in Grand Junction. We ate our lunch and then walked to the movie theater. Carol Norgren John recalled that we watched a Francis the Talking Mule movie starring Donald O'Connor with the young viewers most impressed with the mule. After the movie, the weary children and teachers journeyed back to Rippey, by school bus, a spring field trip to be remembered for many years.

Rippey Depot

Transportation Via School Buses
By Mary Dorris Weaver interviewing Diane Hoskinson Ostrander

The Rippey Consolidated School was opened in 1921. There were 286 pupils. There were 6 bus routes: northwest, southwest, south central, northeast, west central, and southeast. The first country children were to be picked up promptly at 7:30. Bus rules included, "Each bus driver is instructed to stop his bus and see that it is properly flagged across all railroad tracks. He is also ordered to drive at a safe speed and at no time to exceed 20 miles per hour. Every precaution will be taken to guard the welfare of the children, both physically and morally."

The school bus drivers for the Rippey Consolidated School prior to forming a merger with East Greene in 1962 apparently are all deceased.

An interview with Diane Hoskinson Ostrander, who drove a school bus for East Greene in the Rippey Community from 1974-1989, for 15 years, reveals a lot about rural transportation of school children in the 1970's. Diane's route began in Grand Junction, where she drove to the bus barn. She picked up her first student passengers (for a total of 50) at 7:15, with the route being about 35 miles. The route ran in the eastern and southern portion of the rural Rippey community. She dropped off the Rippey area students at the Rippey Center, and then drove to Grand Junction to provide transportation for the elementary students from the northern part of the district back to the Rippey Center. The process was reversed in the afternoon, with the last student getting off the bus at 4:30 P.M. At that time East Greene ran 5 bus routes, and when she began driving they were all driven by women, with the exception of the supervisor.She drove the activity buses for the high school including football, music, and basketball.

She was recruited to become a driver by Mr. Bob Cummings, then transportation director for East Greene. She studied for her chauffeur's license, took the written test, and then had a required driving test. She passed the first time and became an East Greene driver in 1974.

She prides herself on only being stuck in the snow once, and credits that record with always proceeding with caution, driving slowly, and keeping her mantra the same as the one in 1921: the safety of the children.

The largest bus she drove had a capacity of 66, but she drove smaller buses, too, especially with the mid-day transportation of the kindergarten classes at East Greene. She shares a story that during his ride home, one kindergarten boy expressed that he was going to marry her when he grew up.

When she first began driving there were no cell phones nor C.B. radios in the buses. She always told the children departing the bus during a snowstorm, that if a snow accident should happen to the bus, their parents could help by identifying the approximate location when calling for aid.

Diane always talked to her riders during adverse weather, reminding them she needed to focus on her driving and not be looking in her mirror regarding bus mischief. Throughout the interview she praised her student riders for being such good passengers.

She had one kindergarten student who really disliked school and was frequently ill just as he was arriving. She carried an ice cream bucket for vomiting incidences for him, and frequently gave him a little pep talk about facing the day. His mother told her at his high school graduation celebration, he never would have attended school had it not been for Diane.

She notes the decision to cancel school was made in the early morning hours by the superintendent and the transportation supervisor. Every winter she purchased a box of large garbage bags that she retained in the bus, thinking that she and students could wear them for insulation and warmth should an accident occur, and they became stranded.

She said she occasionally purchased treats for her students as a thank you for their being such good passengers.

A 1966 East Greene graduate, Diane fondly recalls driving the bus, "It was one of the best times of my life; people were always so nice to me."

Al Bell Day at School
By Phyllis McElheney Lepke

If you heard the tolling bells today, you might still remember the excitement of what came next. After his signature bells, Al Bell and his wife launched into school assembly programs that amazed and amused elementary students around the State of Iowa for 30 years (1949-79).

The Bells traveled every year (international trips every other year) for six weeks and made their own 16 mm films of what they saw and did. Then they spent the rest of the summer editing the material into programs, which Rhea marketed.

For Rippey grade schoolers like me, these far-away, exotic places were made real by the Bells, who wore costumes from the year's location, displayed artifacts typical of the region, and even sang or danced to convey the lives of those about whom they were talking. Al was the consummate showman.

Do you have a favorite Al Bell program? My husband's is the Everglades program where one of Bell's daughters was filmed diving into water that potentially was home to alligators. The whole family participated in making the films exciting!

When I talk with friends who grew up in other school districts, what we have in common is Al Bell Day. The assembly, which originally cost the schools $10, was presented in as many as 500 locations in one year. Sometimes there were four programs a day; Al was committed to reaching as many young people as possible.

Nostalgic for the Al Bell Day of your childhood? The State Historical Museum of Iowa, Des Moines, is the resting place for much of the Bells' memorabilia. And Becky Bell-Greenstreet wrote a book about her dad (available on Kindle) called, *Al Bell Remembered*.

You will be reminded of a gentler time when we children were still captivated by seeing the state capitol or dining at Bishop's cafeteria, both in "faraway, big city" Des Moines. You will realize that the Bells opened up a world of places that you had barely heard of and took you to many places that stirred your imagination. Weren't we lucky that Al Bell and his family were Iowans!

School Announcements
By Pat Grow McPherson
I remember line rings for school announcements such as snow days! Later in high school when I was dating my later husband I would pause after Steve hung up and would hear click, click, click as people listening in would hang up.

Stop Sign
By Mary Fry Liebich
I can't remember if we were in junior high or high school, but the older kids were designated to help the younger ones get across the street at Radebaugh's corner (across the street from where the parsonage is now). We had vests to wear and a "stop sign" to carry. We would stand on the corner and when younger kids came, we would walk out into the street with our stop sign and halt the traffic. Then the younger ones would cross the street. I don't think there was a stop sign on the corner at that time.

Holey Jeans
By Phyllis McElheney Lepke
I remember when Rippey moms ironed patches on our jeans to cover the rips and tears. Now those holey jeans are fashionable and costly.

Minnesota Woolen Lady
By Mary Ann Bardole Hick
I remember the lady that came to our house with bags of new clothes to sell. I called her the Minnesota woolen lady!

Jack the Milkman
By Mary Ann Bardole Hick
I remember Jack the milkman. Delivered 4 gallons of milk a week for us! Then bought my flute from him!

Farewell To The Rippey School,

1921-2012

The walls will cry,
And so will I,
As children go from here.

No bells will ring,
Or children sing,
When school days end for all.

The building stands,
As many hands,
Found learning through these doors.

Yet time for friends,
Will never end,
For students young and old

The lights go out,
No one's about,
Yet memories live on.

Nancy Bardole Hanaman
May 23, 2012

Student at
Rippey Consolidated School, 1951-1962

The Walls Came Down:
Farewell to the Rippey School Building
Dedicated to students, parents, teachers and those who had
the vision to lay the corner stone in 1920

Drive by slowly,
Once proud school,
Now a stark brick shell,

As the building fell,
Memories flood in.
Days gone by,
Young children venture forth
Kindergartners head to the second floor,
High School kids march on to the floor above.

Memories wander through the ghost of hallways
Into the old gym.
First day of school,
End of the year picnic and games.
Box socials,
Families gathered for PTA meetings.
Class with the most parents attending
Won a prize.

My mother came to this place
A young school teacher,
Met a young banker at Epworth League,
Watched his car glide past en route to lunch.
A newcomer stayed 59 years.

Proud building stood tall,
On the edge of town.
Rising on the rich black soil.
Bricks and mortar clung together
Building a home for young learners.

Generations trod the uneven steps,
To enter the hallowed halls,
Children, teachers, parents.
Music echoes from the vacant band room,
Basketball players charge down the court,
From 6th grade Lions Club Games to High School youth.
My sister, Sharon, fast as a speeding bullet,
More points than any others.

My heart breaks as the walls come down,
Not just the building but a lifetime of memories,
A place always there when we journeyed from distant places.
Brick by brick and load upon load of refuse,
Make the journey to places unknown,
The cathedral of learning
Reduced to a grass graveyard.

Nancy Bardole Hanaman
Oct. 4, 2014

Photograph by Janice Kuehl Harbaugh   June 2020

Notes

Sports Memories

An Element of the Mural Painted in Rippey, Iowa
By Sarah Stotts   Summer 2020

Rippey Was Long A Baseball Town
By Robert Huber

I do not know exactly when I became a baseball fan but I do remember trying to hit green walnuts the first day I went to kindergarten. Dad told some stories about Lester Zanotti and Danny Peters. I was honored to see both of them a few years ago. I enjoyed the times we went to the game on the fourth of July with the fireworks and seeing games under the lights.

The baseball players from Rippey were like heroes to me. My first organized baseball was when I was eight years old and went to Pee Wees in a white t-shirt and jeans. My first coach was a young guy named Pat Daugherty. A book I recently purchased and donated to the Rippey Library gives an excerpt about his teaching position in Rippey. The book tells about his experiences at Indian Hills and I rejoice I found it.

Pat would put me in to pitch a couple of games. I would walk the first two batters and out to center field I would go. I have wondered all these years why he did that? One of the great experiences I had in athletics was playing for Charlie Tipton because he always believed in me and was so kind with praise and support. The only home run I ever hit until my senior year in high school was in Little League. It was thrilling to run the bases in a handed down baseball uniform with an R on my chest.

My favorite teacher in high school was Mel Murken, who taught American history, something I was to do for nine years. During my freshman year I was privileged to play spring baseball with Dave Chase and Harvey Rice and other good athletes. In the spring of my sophomore year we did not have spring baseball and I went out for track. I was pretty good at track but I decided I would rather run on the baseball field. So during the year prior to my junior year I initiated a petition to resume spring baseball.

In a school board meeting it was brought to a vote and it lost 4 to 1 but thanks to my Dad for supporting me. We learned that Mel Murken would be leaving after that summer, so we decided to have Mel Murken Night when we played Jefferson High School.

The year before Steve Fagen had pitched a no-hitter and a one-hitter vs. Jefferson. My junior year he was out of town at game time. We started that game by immediately getting behind either 8 to 1 or 8 to 0. Then it started to rain lightly. I begged Jack Anderson to not call the game.

The Jefferson pitcher began to slip and slide on the mound and walked several batters and we came up with some key hits. Coach Murken put me in to pitch in the 4th and 5th innings. Even though the Rams hit some rockets they went right to people like Mike Thompson at second base and Craig Eilbert in center field. We ended up winning the game 18 to 8 in five innings, the greatest athletic thrill I ever experienced as a player. We had won one for the coach!

I was privileged to be an assistant/sophomore baseball coach for Lou Koenigsfeld at Charles City. I know that at least three of our players played for Pat Daugherty at Indian Hills. His eldest son, Ron, was drafted and played in the minor leagues for a time. When Ron came home from school he told Lou that we could improve on some maintenance issues for the field that he had learned from Pat Daugherty.

We did not have a VW to drag the field, but we did use a small John Deere tractor and made a couple of devices to work on the pitching mound. Ironically, like Coach Daugherty who built fields at Indian Hills, we help build what became Lou Koenigsfeld baseball field in Charles City. I was blessed to have contact with three Iowa Hall of Fame baseball coaches: Pat Daugherty, Mel Murken, and Lou Koenigsfeld and a Hall of Fame baseball umpire, Jack Anderson.

I am grateful to all the Rippey folks who made baseball a part of my experience, people like Walt Anderson, LeRoy Overman, and Jake Peters. I hope you check out the book, *Community Treasure* by Phil Janssen and Jerry Tapp about Pat Daugherty, you will know that a part of Rippey went on with him, and Pat inspired us.

Foul Ball Money
By Mary Fry Liebich
The baseball park again. If a player hit a foul ball that went out of the park past the third base line or past the first base line into where the cars were parked, the kids would get it and take it to the announcer, who would give them 5 cents for bringing it back. The little slot they put the return ball in so that the umpire could pick it up is still there in the stadium. Bring in a couple of foul balls and you'd have enough money to get something from the food stand.

Foul Balls
By Linda Young
I remember chasing after foul balls at Rippey Demons' games. That dime we got for dropping the ball into the grandstand slot felt like big bucks!

Buckeye Coal Mine Baseball Team 1905
By Matthew Lepke, grandson of Jean McKelvey McElheney

The love of baseball spans generations in my family. The man in the center of this photo, my great-great uncle, Mick Feith, played in Rippey for the Buckeye Coal Mine team over 115 years ago. The team was sponsored by the mine, which was owned by my great-great grandfather, Mike Feith.

My grandma, Jean McElheney, used to tell stories of trips in the 1930s that her father, Charles McKelvey, took to Chicago to watch baseball games at Wrigley Field and Comiskey Park.

During the first time I visited Wrigley, in the late 1990s, I thought of him and how--over 60 years later--I was seeing a game at the same ballpark. Carrying on the family tradition, I've now visited over 60 major- and minor-league ballparks across the country, from Asheville, Albuquerque, and Atlanta, to Philadelphia, El Paso, San Diego, and many points in between.

Buckeye Coal Mine Baseball Team 1905
The team was sponsored by the Buckeye Coal Mine owned by Matthew Lepke's great-great grandad Mike Feith. The ball field was southwest of Rippey, near where "Old Rippey" was located.

Front row, L to R	Bert Lovejoy, 1st base
	Mick Feith, pitcher
	Bill Bedwell, catcher
Back row, L to R	Rudolph Fogle, 3rd base
	Frank Johnson, right field
	Otis Rohrer, 2nd base
	Bill Guthrie, center field
	Dick Anschutz, substitute
	Ralph Bayard, left field
	Emanuel States, short stop

This is a copy of the original picture given to Matt Lepke, Christmas 1998, by Matt's grandmother, Jean McElheney

Sports, Sports, Sports
By Jim Fouch

From my earliest years, it was sports. Pick up baseball games, pick up football games, pick-up basketball games. All within walking or biking distance even at the age of 5 and beyond. Games at the baseball field for baseball and football about ¼ mile from home. Many times with my brother Bill, who was 5 years older, (much to his chagrin, as I'm sure he thought of it as babysitting) and others older than I. But if I pouted about getting the crap kicked out of me, I was told to sit down. Really didn't want that to happen! Later, basketball at I.J. Burk's slab at their household garage. The south side of which had at least 4' drop off (maybe it was like 4") within 10' of the basket. Many of the players of these games were repeat participants like Crumley, Killam, Gilroy, Drake, Fouch, DeMoss, Smith, Bardole, Young and many more that I don't recall at this time. After the "new" gym was built in '57, it didn't take long for someone (Roger?) to figure out entrance without a key. The games were shifted to that better location and many times we would be "discovered" by faculty or custodial only to be told to "lock up" when we left.

This was my reason for going to school, to play games. If it involved a ball, I was interested. Classwork, not so much. A funny thing happened along the way though. Because of the patience and persistence of all the teachers, education and a desire to learn rubbed off on me. It was because of teachers like Johnson, Wilson, Crumley, Osborn, Peters, Daugherty, Roberts, Killam, Fry and others, I became especially interested in math and science. A lot of that initially was an interest to be eligible academically for sports, but as time went on, it turned into a real desire to learn.

While in high school, because of Roger Crumley, Carl Killam, Ron Ridnour and others, I started thinking of the possibility of college. No one in our family had ever gone beyond high school. I had no frame of reference for that one. These guys talked like it was a foregone conclusion. I began thinking that way too.

There were about 70 students in the high school, grades 9 – 12 while I was there. A large majority would go on to become Doctors, Nurses, Lawyers, Accountants, Educators, Business people and others with advanced degrees. I believe this was considerably a higher percentage of college attendees than other schools of that era. This was the environment in the Rippey school system. It rubbed off even to those of us who didn't care about education. When you thought all you wanted to do was play ball, be in the band, sing in the choir, and hang out with your friends, without an initial interest in doing so, you became interested in knowledge.

When in college I was pleased to find out I could compete not only on the court, but especially in the classroom. Thank you, Rippey Consolidated School, for making it possible for a start-up, mediocre student like me to become one truly interested in knowledge.

Education, Education, Education

Lucky to Grow Up in Rippey
By Roger L. Crumley (RHS 1960)

I was born two months before Pearl Harbor day. Accordingly, most of my childhood was post WWII. I remember such things as going with my class up on the roof of the schoolhouse, with binoculars, and being trained to look for (enemy, I presume) aircraft. Living at the west end of Main Street, my commute to school was shorter than most. (But why, then, was I so frequently late?!).

One of my vivid memories was looking out to the south late one night, across the ballpark, and seeing flames and smoke high in the sky, as the Stevens and Son Sale Barn burned to the ground. My dad was an auditor or bookkeeper for the huge sales events at that facility, and he had just returned around midnight from a sale there, when we saw the flames.

I also remember working summers during high school at the Rippey Grain Elevator. That was a great job! That too had burned down, but one of the summers (~1958) where I worked for the Elevator (days), I was able to get hired nights also in the construction of the new concrete replacement grain elevator. Those were long 24-hour days!!

But much about Rippey for me, my brothers Phil and Dave, and my parents, Dwight and Helen Crumley, was about sports. Who could forget the old gymnasium with the balcony (which led to the school lunchroom during the day)? As a small boy I watched both of my older brothers playing basketball in that "crackerbox" gym, and they both became role models for me. Then came the great team with Dan Peters, Kent Burrell, Rod Metzler, Earl Comer, and several other excellent players. That year (1955, I believe) the State of Iowa had thrown all big schools together with little schools (no longer any class "B"), and of course, our great undefeated team had to play powerhouse Ames in the Sub-State at Ames, where they lost. Fortunately, Rippey built a big new gym before I started high school in 1956.

But Rippey was decidedly a Baseball Town. My dad played on the Rippey semi-pro "town team" and was catcher for my pitcher-uncle Raymond Crumley. The stories abounded. I still have a scorebook for that team from the 1920 season. My brothers were both good baseball players. (I learned what a no-hitter was at age 7 when brother Phil threw one against Perry!) And who could forget Rippey's great ones Les Zanotti and Dan Peters?

I don't think my Dad ever missed a Rippey game, whether it be "midgets", little league, high school, or "town team" (which was the Rippey Demons name by the time I got to that age). There were so many memorable mornings and afternoons at the ballpark. In the summer about 7 to 15 of us would gather at the park and have "pick-up" games. Many days, we'd go home for lunch, and then come back and play all afternoon. Players from that time frame included Larry Munson, Lynn Wilson, Jerry and Dick Young, Lloyd DeMoss, Larry Gilroy, Carl Killam, Butch Smith, Jim Fouch, and his older brother Billy Joe Fouch. Boy, do I remember Billy Joe Fouch and his fastball AND his curve (which is the main reason I learned to bat left-handed). His curve invariably started right at your head, if you were a right-handed batter!

Larry Gilroy, Don Drake, and I were all Class of '60. We were SO lucky that around 1956, the school hired a young new coach, Patrick Daugherty. Pat came from Cumberland, Iowa, and was a standout baseball and basketball player. He then attended Simpson College on a baseball scholarship. Rippey and all of us benefited tremendously from his skill, enthusiasm, and intricate knowledge of both baseball and basketball. Pat loved baseball, and Rippey, and the ballpark. He had a little yellow Volkswagen bug, and would "drag" the infield with it before every game. I believe he also did the lime-marking of the foul lines as well--everything to make the park look at its best. (And since it was such a great, flat, ballfield, which had had lights installed in 1948 long before most other parks in the state, it hosted several State Tournament final games.)

I'll never forget the caper (this now during basketball season) when Larry, Don, probably Jerry Groves, John Bardole, and myself, and who knows who else.....decided that Coach Daugherty's little VW bug should be turned sideways (making it impossible for him to get out of the parking lot.) So, we simply went out, lifted it up, and turned it 90 degrees, accomplishing our goal.). Pat Daugherty, as many know, went on to become baseball director and coach at Indian Hills Junior College in Centerville IA, (Google "Pat Daugherty Field") where his wisdom, passion for baseball, and incredible people skills enabled him to coach, grow, and graduate several players who were successful in pro ball, including no less than 14 major leaguers. Pat himself later became Chief Scout for the Montreal Expos, and later the Colorado Rockies. Pat's coaching enabled Don and me to play baseball at Simpson, while Larry Gilroy attended and pitched for Buena Vista College.

Indeed Rippey, Iowa, was just a terrific place to have grown up!

Community Treasure
By Pat Daugherty

I, like most kids, wanted to be a big-league ball player and once that was out of the picture, I wanted to coach. After graduating from Simpson College in 1958, I started searching for my first teaching/coaching position. I sent my credentials to the Rippey School and within a few days I got a call from Supt. George Roberts, who invited me for an interview. After seeing the school and the town, I was convinced that this would be a great job. It was a great baseball town with a new school and a well-kept, lighted baseball field. After another brief wait, I was offered a contract for the 1958-59 school year. My first contract was for $2,900. I was head basketball, head baseball, junior high basketball, boys P.E., seventh and eighth grade science teacher and high school general Science and Biology teacher.

I also handled the summer baseball program which consisted of a Midget Team, a Babe Ruth Team and the town's semi-pro team, The Rippey Demons, for which they gave me an additional $200. So, I walked away with $3,100 that first year. Our rent was only $45 per month and I was driving a VW, so I thought we were making a pretty good living. While at Rippey, I started commuting to Des Moines to work on my Master's Degree on Saturdays and during the summer mornings.

Our high school faculty was a close-knit group. Some of them started their teaching careers at the same time I did– George Whaley, Dick Fry, Harold and Rowena Woodward. Of course, the great Jake Peters was the principal and anchor for the staff. Also Mrs. Killam was the English teacher.

I started my second year at Rippey in 1959 and loved every minute of each day during that year. Our first child Mary was born. As I was to begin my fourth year at the school, 1961-62, I was recalled into the service and reported to Fort Carson, Colorado, for a year of active duty with the U.S. Army. While I was serving, the reorganization of school districts was taking place and when I returned for the 1962-63 school year, Rippey was in the East Greene School District with the High School in Grand Junction.

Due to being recalled into the U.S. Army, I was assured a position in the new reorganized school at Grand Junction where I taught biology and was head boys' basketball and assistant baseball coach for the 1962-63 year. The following year I took a job as Head Baseball Coach at Garrigan High School in Algona, Iowa, in northern Iowa where I stayed two years and finished my Master's in Education Degree and was ready to find something more challenging than high school coaching.

We now know Mr. Daugherty went on to Indian Hills Community College in Ottumwa and became a scout for the Montreal Expos and the Colorado Rockies, retiring in 2015. He and his wife JoAnn reside in Centennial, Colorado.

Manager Pat Daugherty arrives home and is greeted by his wife JoAnn and daughter Mary Beth, who see him infrequently in the summer unless they go to the ballpark.

Des Moines Register, June 11, 1961

Basketball Games
By Linda Young

One of my first memories of, well, anything was going to basketball games in the old Rippey gym with my parents.

I was 3 or 4 years old in the mid-1950s and I recall we would head for the balcony to watch my short but savvy sister, Mary Ann (Young) Miller and equally short and savvy cousin, Jean (Young) Spradley, try to help the Bulldogs win some games.

Well, they would watch and I, um, wouldn't, even though I might have wanted to.

Our seats for every game (I thought they must be assigned) were directly behind the old wooden backboard attached to the balcony on the side of the court. I was always planted between mom and dad so, while they paid close attention to the game below, all I ever saw was the wrong side of the backboard. But I'm sure the games were all terrific.

Luckily for me the beautiful school addition was then under construction and would be completed before either of my athletic relatives graduated, so I did enjoy seeing them play in the spacious new confines.

But I often wondered why my parents would plant me somewhere where I couldn't see anything.

Decades later I found the answer. I was visiting in town, dropped by the school and peered into the gym below.

Sure enough, the old backboard was still there as was the railing which, I soon realized, was constructed in such a way that it would have been very easy for a small child to fall through to the floor below. That certainly wouldn't have been good for my health and might have distracted from the game!

Anyway, I've taken away two things from the experience. One, Paul and Betty Young were indeed pretty good parents and, two, Rippey had a terrific school.

Happy birthday No. 150 to my wonderful hometown.

Photograph of Ned High from school annual

A Baseball Prayer
By Pat Daugherty

It's important to me Lord; to some, it's only a game that will be forgotten when they leave the park.

To those of us that have sacrificed countless hours of precious time that you have granted us on your earth, it becomes more important.

We don't expect you to swing the bat or handle the gloves for us Lord, but we do ask that you make us aware of the ability that you have bestowed upon us.

Please don't let us allow this gift to pass on unnoticed.

We ask that when the time comes when we no longer have fun displaying the skills that you bless so few of us with, that we will at least have the courtesy and courage to put our suits away.

Lord, we thank you for the courage, the strength, the ability, and speed to perform for those that are appreciative of this rare ability that you have bestowed upon us.

In your name we ask this, Amen.

Notes

Life on the Farm

An Element of the Mural Painted in Rippey, Iowa
By Sarah Stotts   Summer 2020

Neighbors Helping Neighbors Is A Part Of Rural Iowa Life
By Carol Thompson Sieck

I suppose there are many reasons I am not very good at social media. All things "computer" seem difficult. It is quite likely my age is a factor, but I also suspect there is a cultural influence in my social media stumbles. I was raised in a world where people communicated by talking to one another.

I remember with fond clarity growing up on our family farm southwest of Rippey and feeling like my family was a part of a larger family, a family of neighbors. That larger family provided almost all of our social development skills, or lack of them. There were families with kids my age all around us. The Young family lived across the road. The McElheney twins lived across the field from us. Families surrounded us, the Morse family, the Grow family, the Derry family, the Borgeson family, the Muir family. Also the McCurdys, Morses, Robsons, and Montheis. And it wasn't just that they lived nearby, they were an active part of almost every aspect of our lives.

We kids all rode to and from school together every day. Our parents shared tools and farm implements. Our mothers formed their own neighborhood clubs in order to add an opportunity for the women to discuss community events from a female perspective. Our fathers baled hay together, sorted livestock together, castrated pigs together and pitched in any time one of them was in need of an extra hand. We worked together all through the week and then on Saturday night it was very likely these same families would finish their chores, get their Saturday night bath, and gather together at one home or another for an evening of crazy eights or pinochle around basement card tables while the kids played games upstairs. The week was complete when all these folks would gather once more in church on Sunday morning. Then the cycle would start again.

But the point of all this is that we did it all without texting or email or voice messaging. Of course, we didn't have those options either. But did we need them? I know they are a convenience, and they somehow fit into my life today, but I'm glad I didn't have them as a child. I think I would have missed a lot.

In 1956 I was six years old. To my best recollection I believe there were at least thirty-five families that lived within two miles of our rural Rippey farm home. We all filled each other's needs and some of those needs were extreme. The spring of 1956 provided one of those extreme examples because it was about April of that year that we lost two large barns to a fire.

We kids had been to Perry with Mom to get groceries and we could see the smoke from the Perry airport not yet knowing the catastrophe was ours. Various kinds of hardship had always been part of farm life but we were shocked at the fire's devastation. Even more shocking, however, was what happened after. More than thirty-five, that's right, 35 men gathered within one week's time to complete the cleanup of debris and construction of a new barn, a genuine, old-fashioned barn raising.

And it wasn't just men. Entire families came. Children played in the yard and women prepared meals large enough to feed an army. Everyone pitched in. Everyone helped us just like we all helped each other. Doesn't that seem amazing?

I know progress is good and necessary, but so is human contact. Tapping a Facebook "thumbs up" is just not the same as getting together with friends and neighbors to accomplish something good. Gardening together, sewing together, playing together, laughing together is still way better than Twitter. In short, I guess I'm satisfied with my social media limitations. I guess I'll have to rely on plain old person-to-person socializing instead. It seems like that's more how I was raised.

Build Barn On Thompson Farm

The Darwin Thompson farm was the scene of another good neighbor day Saturday when over 35 men gathered at 8 o'clock to construct a 40x90 foot Doane pole barn to replace buildings that were destroyed by fire the previous Saturday.

Monday following the fire, good neighbors cleaned up the lots and H. S. Stevens furnished the caterpillar and bulldozer with which two 7-foot ditches were dug, to bury the debris, make the necessary fill and cover the old foundation.

Pictured after four hours of construction, is the frame work of the large building which will be inclosed on three sides with car siding, creosoted about 4 feet high. A door on the east end, with driveway through the center of the building will allow feed to be hauled to bunks. The roof is of corrugated steel. A 24x60 foot hog barn will be built later.

Evergreen trees in the yard were scorched. Paint on the crib, garage and the trim on the stucco house was blistered by the heat of the fire.

Among those men who helped in this good neighbor project were those whose names were listed by the news reporter as the group ate

Tom Grow, Dwight Muir, Vern Derry, Dale Morse, Jack McElheney, Noah Thompson, Howard Kenny, Eldon Grow, Dave Kirk, Warren Mount, Bill Armstrong, Harvey Morse, Ivan Burk, Wayne Thompson, Ralph Hane.

Charles Newhouse, Darwin Culley, Lawrence Huber, Harold Grow, Don Griffin, Bill Monthei, Darwin Grow, John Grow, Owen Lape, Glenn Grow, Darwin Johnston, Merle Coon, Leonard Myers, Dale Joy, Leonard Robson, Elmer Young and Donald Grow.

Ladies who assisted Mrs. Thompson and her mother-in-law as they served the dinner were: Mrs. Leonard Robson, Mrs. Owen Lape and Glenda and Mrs. Ralph Hanes. Among others who furnished food were: the Mesdames Harold Grow, Eugene Muir, John Grow, Noah Thompson, Darwin Johnston, Bill Monthei, Vern Derry, Jack McElheney, Merle Coon, Howard Kenny, Harvey Morse, Charles Hanes, Lloyd Winkleman and Alberta Bardole.

Church in Rippey
By CaroleAnne Souder Vannoy

My granddaughters love to hear my stories of growing up on the farm in a rural community, which is something they have yet to experience. What I find myself coming back to time and again is the feeling of security we shared.

All of my memories are centered around church, school and family. My earliest memories are of the love I received from Mary Bardole and Lila Johnston in the church nursery when I was confused by the fact that I had a treasured red plastic bear at home and they had the exact bear at church. Completely sure that they had MY bear, I held tightly to it. There was never a raised voice or even a scowl. Is it any wonder that I loved church?

I remember the kitchen in that same building being used to make raised donuts. The chatter sprinkled with laughter and imbued with the smell of donuts frying up in a row of electric skillets made for a cheery environment. That same building was used for our Sunday School classes.

Something I always looked forward to was Darlene Morse asking me to sit with her. Being a year younger than her made that twice as special. I can still feel the rough canvas cover of our little blue children's hymnals. Oh, the joy of being the one who picked the next hymn! I always knew what Darlene would pick if she was chosen: This is My Father's World. Sometimes I would pick it for her because I knew how happy it would make her. This would be the first hymn I taught my own children and I still sing it when life seems uncertain.

One of my fondest memories is of Sue Diehl being my Sunday School teacher. She was beautiful inside and out.

Her gentle ways made each of us feel welcomed. One lesson that still means a lot to me was one she shared on the importance of names in the Bible. She concluded the lesson by telling each of us what our name meant. She told me mine meant "song of joy" and that she knew it was most certainly true of me. I took that to heart and I credit her with putting me on the path to being an optimist.

Another happy memory was being to church on time to help LeRoy Overman ring the church bell. LeRoy always smelled of aftershave, and I cannot think of even one time that it didn't seem his smile came all the way from his toes. He even walked in a cheerful way.

The other profound memory I have of the old church building is the whisper of hand fans over the pastor's words, the way the sounds filled the church when we sang hymns together, the quiet silence of the sanctuary if you were the first to arrive or the last to leave, and the glory of light streaming through the stained glass.

I don't remember what we called the church building to the south but I remember several rummage sales being organized by the church ladies in there. After the new church was built, I would have to say that most of my church memories involve food: soup suppers, potlucks, socials, weddings, showers and such. It seemed that we had meals together regularly, but more important, we did the work together. I remember all the fathers and grandfathers cranking ice cream makers out in the summer heat for our ice cream socials. Then there were tables filled with slices of cake and pie to go with the ice cream. Admittedly I resented clearing the table and washing dishes at home, but at church it felt completely different. I saved up all the kind words about how thoughtful and diligent I was like nuggets of gold. In that kitchen are all my most tender memories of being loved and appreciated.

I also have fond memories of Sunday School and Vacation Bible School. It seemed that Velda DeMoss and Jean Borgeson led every singing group for us kids. Can anyone forget their infectious laughter? The kids I teach Bible to now will ask for my "old" songs. My favorite one to share is Sunshine Mountain.

My own favorite Bible teachers were Jake Peters, Paul Bardole and Myron Rinker. Paul and Jake were so engaging because they spoke from their hearts. I never remember them reading from a lesson, and I crafted my own teaching style based on theirs: know the topic well and share it enthusiastically.

I love Myron for completely different reasons. By the time he was my teacher, I was a hardened skeptic and I venture to guess a bit of a pain in the backside. Yet he was there for me every Sunday patiently addressing my questions of faith. We chuckled about those struggles over coffee at the Perry HyVee not so long ago. I am most assuredly glad he can laugh about it, and I am ever more glad that faith triumphed over skepticism.

Another treasured memory is going through Confirmation Class with my peers. Previous to this class I took great pride in being the first to raise my hand whenever a question was asked. But I found myself completely stumped when the pastor asked who could say the books of the Bible. Not me. Truth be told I still can't. Good to be humbled now and again.

I wish I had a picture from Vacation Bible School so you could see what a joyful church looks like. I remember families who didn't send their kids for Sunday School would send their kids to VBS, so we were bursting from the seams. What stands out most vividly are memories of all the moms and grandmas pitching in to make every moment memorable. There were new songs, bountiful snacks to be washed down with Kool-Aid, and crafts galore. I could wax eloquent for hours, but I will close by saying thank you to all those who made church a wonderful place to grow up. I hope a lot of my friends and family will also share their memories. We were blessed to grow up together.

Climb, climb up sunshine mountain
Heavenly breezes blow;
Climb, climb up sunshine mountain
Faces all aglow.
Turn, turn from sin and doubting,
Look to God on high,
Climb, climb up sunshine mountain
You and I.
Traditional Hymn

Rippey's Legacy of Plowing Champions
By Robert Huber

Mary Weaver has asked me for my recollections of the 1996 National Plowing Matches held on our family farm, near Rippey, Iowa. As much I thought I had remembered, I have forgotten, so up to the attic I went to find my Dad's history of plowing matches. The contests originally were scheduled for far western Iowa, but after much previous optimism no site could be secured. Dad told the Iowa Plowing Association that he had 64 acres of hay ground that could be plowed, so in a rather last minute fashion the matches came to Rippey.

Some fifty-three (53) contest plots were plowed in state and national contests on September 5, 6, and 7. All the plots had to be staked out prior to the contests, including practice areas. Contestants were from several parts of Iowa, including the local boys, Steve King and Roger Norgren. The National contestants were from Illinois, Iowa, Minnesota, Ohio, Pennsylvania, and South Dakota. There were four categories of National contests including small plow, large plow, classic, and antique. The winners of the small plow and large plow would be eligible for the World Contest the following year.

It is estimated that 500 people attended the contests, a little smaller than the 150,000 who had attended Agri-rama at Jefferson in 1966. But the plowing conditions were great thanks to good weather and a great alfalfa crop. Dad's small machine shed became headquarters for the plowmen. Every morning there was a short prayer service, and it was headquarters for eating and plowing meetings. His large shed was used to find plowing equipment the plowmen needed to borrow. The garage served as a nursing situation should it be needed. I laugh at a picture I have in the garage of Connie Neese taking Dad's blood pressure as he could get nervous!!!

The west end of the farm field was used to organize the equipment and tractors. The ditch and driveways were used to unload and reload the trucks of equipment. The county oiled the gravel road in front of the farmstead. Prior to the event, Bob Muir provided a meal for the staking crews. The Rippey United Methodist Youth helped with refreshments and drinks on site during the contests.

Dad and Mom wrote a thank you published in the local papers and I will only list the Rippey folks mentioned, but there is also a wonderful list of Greene County contributions as well. This included the Rippey Savings Bank, Steve King Trucking, Rippey Farmers Co-op, the entire Bob Muir family, Brubaker Construction, Myron Rinker, Peoples Bank, Heater and Sons Farms, Roger and Colleen Norgren, Kevin and Haven Hick, Bardole Farms, Inc., Darwin and Ned Johnston, Dale Morse, Rippey United Methodist Youth, Rev. Eric Guy and Rev. Rich King. The Huber family had a full heart as a result of the support of the Rippey community.

Steve King plowed and finished second in the National Small Plow Class in 1996. Steve had won the National Matches in 1986, was a World Contestant representing the United States with one other U.S. plowman in 1987. At the 1988 World Plowing Contests at the Amana Colonies, Steve was selected to plow USA in a plot of land. A Russian plowed USSR. It was a grand sight for aerial photography.

Roger Norgren finished first in the National Large Plow Class using Dad's contest plow in the 1996 contests. It was his second National Championship and he plowed in the World Contest in 1991. Roger elected not plow in a second world contest.

Dad would have liked 20,000 people to attend but most of the guests were familiar with good plowing. He had me daily send the results to WHO radio and report to KDLS. When everyone left for home after those three September days there was nary a can or paper plate to be found on the place.

Rippey has been a plowing contest hub in Iowa over the years as the following folks from Rippey plowed in state and national contests: Merle Coon, Bill Heater, Laurence Huber, Steve King, Bob Monthei, Roger Norgren, and Sterling Young. In the mid 1960's Steve King caught the bug of plowing contests watching the first East Greene FFA contests held in the same Huber field as the 1996 event.

Dad plowed in competitions from 1954 until 1962. He helped a number of plowmen, several who were honored to serve the United States in world competitions. I asked him if he would like to give plowing contests another try in 2004 at Boone in the state plowing contests, 50 years after his first one. One of his pupils beat him by a point or two. But he was able to compete again in Boone in 2005 when he became a National Champion, something he cherished his remaining days. Maybe it helped that he was wearing his Rippey Lions Club cap during the competition or that Jerry Groves hauled his equipment to the site, rather than Dad driving to it.

When Dad placed third in the National Contests in 1962 he won a small amount of prize money. Merle Coon had hauled Dad's tractor and plow to Ohio for the matches and Dad told him he wished he had a trophy instead. Merle got in touch with some folks in Rippey who presented him with the finest of all his trophies and plaques which resided as a center piece of the Huber living room for nearly 50 years. It is these acts of generosity of a small town that makes you proud of your roots.

This photo shows Laurence Huber's contest plow which he first used in 1956, It originally was a 314 number 16 International which he expanded to a 4 bottom and used in the 2004 state match. This photo, taken in the same field used for the national contests in 1996, is likely from 2005 or 2006 after Huber won the national contest. Robert comments, "This is how dad always plowed, like he was in a contest."

Laurence Huber's Contest Plow circa 2006
after winning national contest

Hay Baling Memories
By Duane Coon

During my high school years (1972 to 1975), I hired out a lot to local farmers, most of that for hay baling and corn shelling. Undoubtedly, the most hay baling I ever did for one farmer was for Borgesons and other folks they baled for. When I baled for Borgesons, Karl always drove the tractor pulling the baler and Ralph would do many jobs, including stacking on the rack, hauling to the barn, loading the elevator, or stacking in the hay mow or shed.

Borgesons were some of the hardest workers I was ever associated with. They started early and worked late and didn't take many breaks, except for eating lunch. Karl was a man of very few words. Of all the times I loaded the rack while he pulled the baler, I rarely heard him say much of anything. He reminded me a lot of my Grandpa Neese, who worked the same way. Those guys had a work ethic that revolved around one thing, how much you could get done in a day, and if they did any talking at all it would be at the end of the day to congratulate everyone on how much we accomplished that day.

Karl never complained about the heat, or the bumps, or getting tired. I never once heard him complain about anything unless some of the machinery broke down. Then, he reverted to Swedish, for what I assume was some cussing. Ralph was lighter hearted and more outgoing than Karl. Ralph and I would visit off and on all day long. He enjoyed telling stories and having a good laugh whenever possible.

Borgesons had a lot of hilly ground down by the river, so baling on those slopes could be a real challenge for two reasons: (1) you had to stack the rack just so and "lace" the bales together or the whole darn load would go sliding right off the rack when Karl headed down a slope, and (2) there were always thistles growing on those slopes and those stickery plants would go right through my blue jeans like they weren't even there. On a rare occasion, one could also encounter surprises like a bull snake caught up in a hay bale.

I remember stacking hay in the barns and sheds at the Borgeson home place. They had two little blond-haired boys that always liked to be right in the middle of things. They would often come out to the shed and "help" me move bales. Ralph would usually do the hauling from the field and then, in this case, he would pick those bales up one by one and throw them up into the shed where I was carrying and stacking them. Throwing bales was easily the hardest work of all, because if the hay was getting baled damp, those bales could be mighty heavy and the twines would be real tight on the bale.

Ralph, just like his dad, never complained about anything. We would usually be hot, covered in sweat, and coated with hay dust and pieces, but we took all that in stride. I always looked forward to the dinner bell when Jean would serve up her ham sandwiches and plenty of stuff to go with them.

Sometimes, Borgesons would bale hay for their friend Judge Hanson. The judge was quite a character. Being a Federal judge, he clearly never needed the income from farming, but he dearly loved rolling up his sleeves and doing some good old farming work. Sometimes his younger son would work with us as well. I remember he always drove a little blue convertible sports car. I remember the judge had a barn on his place with a very unusual mow because there wasn't any hard floor in it. Instead, it had some kind of woven wire mesh type of floor. The judge always honored me because he would refuse to bale his hay until I was available to do the stacking on the rack.

Like Borgesons, Judge Hanson had very sloping hay fields and he always claimed that I was one of the few people that could make the loads tie together well enough to stay put on the rack. The judge had known my father, who had the nickname of "Zip", so Judge Hanson often called me Zip or Zipper out of habit, I guess.

Judge Hanson had a club foot, which made it challenging for him to get around, especially on soft hay bales in a mow. When I stacked hay in the judge's barn mow, I remember him climbing up the elevator and telling me that he couldn't walk around on the hay to help me stack, but he would stand at the top of the elevator and throw the bales towards me as far as he could. Judge Hanson always paid me an hourly rate much higher than the going rate. That's just the way he was, he had lots of money and he was generous with it when we helped him farm.

I also remember one lunch break when Judge Hanson and Ralph were asking me what I was going to do for a career when I got out of high school. I remember yet that Judge Hanson said that if I wanted to pursue a military career that he had the ability to give me an appointment to an academy. That was never a path I pursued, but I was honored all the same that he offered it. I also remember Ralph telling me how much the judge's salary and retirement pension were, and we both marveled that he loved getting out and getting dirty and sweaty in the hay mow with the rest of us.

I never knew back then what all a Federal judge did, but I knew he was highly placed. That made it all the more of a surprise one day when he came out with a six pack of Budweiser and asked me, as a 16 year old kid, if I would join him in sitting under the hay rack out of the sun and having a "cold one". I guess the judge knew that "what goes on in the hayfield stays in the hayfield" and he knew he could trust us.

One thing I certainly remember is how tired I would be after baling hay all day with Borgesons. I often came home and fell asleep on the floor. My mother had a mighty difficult time trying to wake me up enough to clean up for bedtime. This hard, back breaking work was a big part of my inspiration when it came time to get serious with high school studies and think about college and a professional career. I pursued a civil engineering degree at Iowa State and I've been engineering projects for big companies ever since, 26 years now. Even now, living in the rolling Ozark hills of Arkansas, I still have fond recollections of my younger days in the hay fields every time I smell some fresh cut hay.

Detasseling
By Mary Fry Liebich

Detasseling was tough work
Wet and cold,
Muddy
And hot,
Almost simultaneously.

Detasseling Memories
By Julene Rittgers Boza

I was 15 in the Summer of 1954 and eager to earn money. My family (Wesley, Mae, and Marna Rittgers) lived in the big Hagerman house on Main Street, next to the highway.

No Taco Bell or McDonalds in Rippey, but thankfully Mrs. Gartsee liked the way I mowed her grass; I did not mow off her flowers like the boys did when they mowed her yard. She was also my piano teacher which probably put me in first consideration for mowing her grass the first time. After not mowing off flowers, the job was mine.

I also mowed grass in Mrs. Amy Kelly's large yard; she had bought the house my parents built when they moved into town from our farm. Myron and Maralynn Rinker own the house now and live there.

Art Todd and his wife Lena hired me to clean their home now and then. Mrs. Todd liked my cleaning abilities, thanks to my mom's teachings. I hung out quilts and bedding on the clothesline for airing and cleaned venetian blinds, in addition to regular cleaning. Art loved my mother's lemon pies; when the girls in my high school class (Class of '57) held bake sales at the Rains grocery store, he was always there early to buy the whole lemon pie.

Summer of 1955, somebody had the great idea of detasseling field corn. Same Somebody said the pay was good. I cannot remember how the idea progressed, but I do recall Sally Burke Drake and I were in the crew – my apologies to other crew members because I am unable to recall all names today. We did not ride the big machines to detassel, we walked the rows of corn. Did I mention we walked the rows?

Our first job was the Dale Roberts farm east of Rippey, (father of my school classmate since Kindergarten, Philip). We were told the corn rows were one mile long, although on some days, they seemed more like five miles long. OK, following thoughts in no particular order:

1. It takes a person with good hardworking peasant stock in their family tree to work in a corn field in the heat of an Iowa summer.

2. Cool, refreshing breezes do not gain access to corn rows. Corn is taller than the person trying to pull the tassel. Pulling tassels will make your hand, wrist, arm, shoulder, and back hurt. No complaining.

3. Only inexperienced teenagers wanting money are eligible to apply.

4. You will get sunburned. Do not apply for this job just because you want a nice tan.

5. You may not quit, call in sick, walk off the job, or die from heat because the farmer planted this darn corn knowing it had to be detasseled and he is depending on you.

6. Remember your folks know this farmer and we do not want to embarrass them by screwing up and pulling tassels off an incorrect row of corn.
7. Start very early, do not let the sun get to the field before you do. Wear long shorts and long- sleeved shirts. In the early morning, corn rows are wet with dew. Half-way down a one-mile row, the dew on your shirt turns to steam and will never dry.

8. Corn leaves are sharp and will cut body parts. My sister Marna Kay remembers my hands were very cut up and hurt like the dickens. My mother, Mae Rittgers-Presnell, took a pair of my dad's socks to fashion gloves for my hands and arms.

9. Do not forget Cool Clear Water. First thing every morning, we would estimate the halfway point of the rows, walk into the rows from the side of the field, and put many jugs of water on the ground at that halfway point. As we pulled tassels working the field, we looked for the jugs. When we came upon the jugs, we knew we were half done with the group of rows we were working on. Cool Clear Water at the beginning of the rows, at the end of the rows, and in the middle of the rows.

10. Pack snacks for the whole crew. My mother made many batches of "Detasseling Cookies". Recipe follows:

> *1/2 c. Carnation milk, 2 c. sugar, 1/2 c. butter. Bring to boil – boil one minute stirring constantly. Add 1 t. vanilla after cooking. Pour over: 3 c. quick oatmeal, 3 T. cocoa, 1/2 c. coconut, and nuts if desired. Drop by teaspoon onto cookie sheet – cool.*

I did make money that summer and was on a good crew;I recall we all got along and did have fun. It was hard work; I could not do that work today. If they still detassel corn in Iowa, would I encourage my granddaughter to sign up? Hmmmm.

Oh, Those Party Lines...
By Phyllis McElheney Lepke

The telephone system in Rippey when I was growing up out in the country consisted of party lines, which meant that several homes were on one phone line and a caller needed to inform the telephone operator of the phone number, so the appropriate number of long and short rings could be rung on the right line. My home phone number was 2 on 99, which meant that two rings (I think they were short.) on line #99 was the way to let us know that someone was calling our house and not my grandmother's which was a different number and length of rings on the same line. There were others on the line as well.

So, when my boyfriend, later my husband Larry, was in the Air Force and stationed in Mississippi, he would eventually reach me after several conversations with the long-distance operators. They simply could not believe that "2 on 99" was a phone number! Every time Larry had to convince them to contact the operator in Rippey, Iowa, and ask that 2 on 99 be rung. Carol Norgren John tells me that she had the same problem trying to call home from college, and Mary Lee Dorris Weaver remembers when Gary tried to call from New York City after returning from Germany.

Of course, since the operator sat on the Main Street in Rippey, she could observe who was in town and what was happening. If you weren't sure someone whom you wanted to call was at home, you could ask the operator if that person was in town. She would tell you if she had seen his/her car go by.

And party lines were the social media of their day. All of the rings were heard on every phone on a single line, so everyone knew when someone else got a phone call. It was common knowledge that the other parties on the line would very quietly pick up the phone, put a hand over the mouthpiece so as not to be heard breathing, and listen in to the conversation. (This was referred to as "rubbernecking.") Larry and I were careful what we said.

Toilet Paper Shortage
By Les Zanotti
Right now, because of the Coronavirus, there is a great shortage of toilet paper nationwide, which would never have been a problem in Rippey because we all had big Sears and Montgomery Ward catalogs.

Grandparents Playing Baseball
By Steven Pearson
This Rippey remembrance is from Steven Pearson, grandson of Dale and Nancy Hanaman. He wrote it when he was 7 years old in 2008 for a school assignment and received a "Good Job" note from his teacher. The unique spelling of Rippey is his.

I go to Rippy, Iowa, every summer. My grandma is very old but she played baseball with me. My grandpa is very old but he played baseball with me, too. There are workers there to make my grandma and grandpa's house bigger.

Two Reflections
By Dale Hanaman

Before Nancy and I were married, we came to the farm near Rippey to spend the weekend. This is where Nancy's parents, Clark and Esther Bardole, and her grandfather, William Huber, resided. It was on or about the fall of 1966.

Being a city boy from Beloit, Wisconsin, I was familiar with a telephone party line for two families. I did have some suspicion of this family – thinking they were quite rude. Some of the time a phone call could be heard and no one answered. Other times when the phone rang, it was answered by one of Nancy's parents. This went on for all of Saturday.

Sunday came, and so did a few phone calls – with the same response as witnessed by me on Saturday. So, I finally asked, "Why is it that sometimes the phone is answered and sometimes not?" Nancy's comment was, "It wasn't our ring." So, I responded, "Well, I heard it ring." Nancy further explained that they shared a party line with several other people, and that their ring was "two longs and three shorts". I still thought this was a strange arrangement, but the explanation was clear.

Clark and Esther Bardole, Nancy's parents, owned a column stick shift 1960 white 4-door Ford Falcon. *This vehicle would become a wedding gift from Nancy's parents to us at the time of our wedding June 8, 1968.*

I had not driven a stick shift car before, so Nancy was giving me pointers on using the clutch. I was getting used to my feet having to not only accelerate and break, but to use my left foot to push in the clutch to change gears.

We went to buy some groceries in Jefferson for Nancy's mom. On our return home, we were stopped by a State Patrol officer doing a random check of cars traveling east out of Jefferson, near the cemetery.

The registration needed to be provided for observation. And then the officer moved around the car to inspect the lights – front and back. Then he said, "Put on the high beams." I turned to Nancy and asked how to do that. She said, "Push down on the small floor button below the clutch." I thought that was a strange place to put the low/high beam button. What if you needed to downshift at the same time the low beam was required? We did end up passing the inspection.

But had it not been for Nancy alongside me, I wouldn't have known where the low/high beam button was located.

Walking Beans and Detasseling
By Mary Fry Liebich

We made our money before we could drive by walking beans and detasseling. I was with a crew detasseling a few times, but I also just walked a certain number of acres for the corn people in Perry (located by the railroad tracks then. Pioneer?)

Anyway, I contracted to do a certain number of acres on a field that is just about 1/4th of a mile beyond the Angus curve as you are going to Perry. It's the field on the north just past the intersection after the curve. I think it was owned by someone named Wicks, but I could be wrong about that. Anyway, I hated that field because you couldn't tell where you were. The house was too far away for you to see the trees, and the telephone or electrical lines which were along the road on the Angus side didn't tell you where you were. I go past the field several times a week and now, 65 years later, still don't like that field.

Sale Barn(s)
By Mary Dorris Weaver

Rippey is known for many things: mining, sale barn auctions, baseball, and the BRR (Bike Ride to Rippey). This remembrance will focus on the livestock and machinery sale barn auctions held in the Rippey community in the 1930's-50's.

Most of this material comes from a presentation completed by the late Velda DeMoss when she gave a program for the monthly meeting of the Greene County Historical Society as it was hosted at the Rippey United Methodist Church. This document covers the auction houses of Stevens and Kelly, and then Stevens and Son. This was originally presented in April of 2005. A full copy of the presentation and pictures are available for review at the Rippey Library.

The sale barn industry in Rippey was started by O. R. (Orrie) Stevens. He had been in the auction business since 1920 when he worked as a "ring man", a person who took bids from individual buyers and then relayed them to the auctioneer. He had deep roots in Greene County as his grandparents settled two miles west of the current town of Dawson.

In 1939 James Kelly and O.R. Stevens built a sales pavilion 1 ½ miles southwest of Rippey, on the east side of what is now Greene County Road P-46. There was seating capacity for several hundred people, and pens and stalls for hundreds of head of livestock. The first livestock sale was held on Monday, August 21, 1939. Machinery was soon added and the business grew until there were two rings outside the building for machinery, as well as livestock in the pavilion. Some days trucks could not unload until the sold livestock was loaded out by the buyer.

The sale began at noon and would often last past midnight. At times over $100,000 was generated by the sales.

Orrie traveled to the western states on the Union Pacific railroad the day following a sale to purchase cattle and horses for the next week. He frequented Nebraska, Wyoming, and Colorado. There were no "rent a car" places, or Ubers, so he hitchhiked between appointments. He paid the ranchers cash for the livestock but denied ever being robbed or seemingly even in danger on these buying excursions. By the end of the week railroad cars of horses and cattle arrived in Grand Junction at the depot livestock pens, to be trucked to the auction pavilion for the next Monday sale.

A café was also housed in the building, called the "Sale in Café." It was only open on sale day. Frequently persons not associated with the sale would come and eat lunch. It had eight booths and a long lunch counter.

The day after Thanksgiving in November of 1947, the barn was destroyed by fire. The partnership dissolved and Orrie went on alone. A former wooden schoolhouse was brought in to serve as the sales office, but there were no further livestock auctions. Since the sale was now handling only machinery, the territory which it served became larger. Machinery was trucked in from Mexico, Mississippi, Colorado, Montana, the Dakotas, Indiana, Ohio, and Kentucky. It enlarged because of the scarcity of machinery following the war, and partially because the Office of Price Administration restricted dealer sale profits. Machinery could be sold at a higher price at the auction than the dealer's business. The Black Market for machinery thrived in Greene County.

Later Orrie formed a partnership with his son Herman and continued the operation as Stevens and Son.

While airplanes were sometimes sold at the sale, LaVere Derry recalls up to six planes sitting in his parents' pasture. They landed on a red clover pasture with a freshly mowed landing strip and taxied to the Derry farm. Those planes were owned by flying farmers who came to purchase machinery.

Orrie divorced, and his former wife married his former partner, Jim Kelly in 1949. In 1950 Jim Kelly built a sales pavilion 1/2 mile south of Rippey. This pavilion and sheds had room for hundreds of head of livestock and seating for several hundred people. Besides the livestock, an addition was added to the north side of the structure allowing cars to be driven past the buyers. There was also a cafe called the Max-Den Café, named for the grandsons of Orrie Stevens.

Jim Kelly died of a heart attack in 1953 and the sale barn went through a series of unsuccessful owners and managers. The Stevens sale barn closed in 1956.

Sale Barn

Stevens & Kelly
Sales Pavilion

Rippey, Iowa

Sales Every Monday

Our Pavilion was started in 1939 and has been given a fine reception. So well has the public liked our work that we have tripled our business in the past year. We are very appreciative.

We Cater to Western Cattle and Hogs Besides our Local Run of Livestock

Lots of Out-of-State Buyers Here Each Week

Up-to-Date Cafe
Mrs. O. R. Stevens, Mgr.

O. R. STEVENS

JAMES KELLY

Notes

Mining

Greene County Coal and Mining Company 1930-1948

Coal Mining And The Zanotti Family
By Gina Zanotti Daley

In 1931 Mac Elvin was drilling a well for water when he discovered a 5 foot vein of coal at 169 feet. This was about one mile south of the current Squirrel Hollow Park. He called a coal salesman to inspect the sample. The end result was the formation of the Greene County Coal and Mining Company. The company was launched with 14 stockholders providing $68,000.00. Joseph Strachan was the major stockholder, having learned the mining business in the British Isles, prior to coming to the U.S. The coal was considered low grade bituminous with 25% ash, twice as much as in eastern coal, but it was good burning coal, and the locality made it desirable as freight costs were much less than if shipped from the East.

Andrew Zanotti traveled from Italy to America with his father in 1909 when he was 13 years old. In Italy, the family had owned large amounts of property prior to WWI, but the government took the land. The plan was for Andrew to earn enough money to bring the rest of his family to America. His father returned to Italy leaving Andrew to learn mining in Missouri. He arrived in Rippey at the age of 33 in 1930. He helped to start the Greene County Coal and Mining Company. At its peak it produced 400 tons of coal per day and provided jobs for nearly 200 persons.

Work began at 8 a.m. and ended at 3:30 primarily during the coolest 9 months of the year. Each miner carried his own lunch and ate his meal in the mine. A miner could carve six tons of coal per day and receive 97 cents per ton. Nearly 100 miners worked underground. Many single miners lived in camps composed of rather poorly constructed temporary housing, but several including Andrew Zanotti, lived in Rippey. The Zanotti family would have to be described as very industrious, as well as creative. Andrew lived in Madrid at the time of the opening of the mine, and lived in Rippey the first year, commuting back to Madrid on the weekends. Upon moving to Rippey, they rented rooms to two or three borders who worked at the mine, and Andy drove them to the mines being paid on a weekly basis. He had a Model T Ford which he used to travel to the mine.

In 1932 he purchased a V-8 Ford, one of two purchased in Rippey, the other one being bought by a local banker.

The mine was about one mile long and 147 feet deep. (Think the width of a football field). Once the corridors were extended three hundred feet away from each side of the main shaft, another corridor would be made at a right angle to the first. Off of these, rooms were made from which the coal was dug.

The miner's room became longer the further in he dug, eventually nearly coming in touch with the miner working in the opposite room. Hundreds of posts had to be placed in staggered positions to prevent the slate or stone room from caving in on the miner.

Andrew laid tracks on which the coal cars traveled. He drilled the holes for the powder and fuses which were used to explode and break down the coal. The tracks extended out of each room and joined main tracks headed toward the hoist at the main shaft. Small mules were used in the mine to pull the cars to where the miners loaded them and to an area where a winch type motor pulled them to the mine shaft. The loaded cars were then hauled to the surface by an elevator type conveyance. Coal could be delivered from the mine to an individual's home for $4.00 a ton. Sometimes as many as 50-60 trucks were in line during the day as well as the night for 24-hour loading.

Most of the coal was used in Greene County, but some was shipped by rail to northern Iowa and southern Minnesota.

The Rippey miners were not union organized, but the Madrid area miners were. Andrew learned that union leaders from Madrid were coming to organize the Rippey area miners. Had they successfully organized, the price of coal would have been raised, and because of its poor quality, the action would essentially put the mine out of business.

In anticipation, Andrew called the sheriff and told him trouble was brewing.

According to a private interview conducted by Gina Zanotti Daley, "When Andrew left for the mine that morning, he had his German Luger stuck inside his waist band. He wasn't looking for trouble, but he was going to be ready. Andrew wasn't one to run away from a fight. About the time he got to the mine, the sheriff also arrived. The union miners arrived from Madrid and piled from their cars. Brewing for a scrap, the sheriff fired a few rounds of ammo into the side of a nearby hill. He told the union miners to get back in their cars and never show their faces again." They complied at that time.

Mining provided a steady employment except in the summer. To supplement his income, some summers Andrew worked for local farmers, and one summer he and his family went to live in Chicago, where he worked as a yard man.

To keep water from building up in the mine, from the springs coming into the mine, water was pumped to the surface through pipes that were located against the side of the mine shaft. Mr. Strachan (the owner) and Andrew were replacing some of those water pipes in the shaft one

Sunday morning. They were using the top of the elevator as scaffolding, and the pipes propped on the surface with lumber and jacks. As they were going down one elevator, the other elevator was coming up. It hit some of the lumber or jacks and knocked them over and the elevator plunged killing the two men. Andrew was 51 years of age; Joseph Strachan was 61. This occurred in 1947.

The miners were not a separate community. Artage did not feel he was ever discriminated against because of being Italian or a coal miner's son. After his father was killed, the community stood behind Mrs. Zanotti and her two sons. She was provided a job in the bank, and whenever Artage or Lester needed summer work, someone always offered a job.

Later that year the tipple (top of mining construction) burned. Gas was beginning to rival coal and the mine subsequently closed in 1948.

My Grandfather's Life in The Coal Mine
By Lynn Wilson

My Grandfather, John Wilson, farmed at different locations and dug tiles around Rippey in the summers during the Depression years. To generate income in the winters to support his wife and four children, he worked as an expert dynamiter in the McElheney coal mine south of Rippey near the gravel pits.

He would get up in the early hours and walk several miles through snow and ice, and sometimes bitter cold, to get to the mine. He would then go down the deep elevator shaft to a small underground tunnel. He would crawl into it and lie on his back, and then dig holes with a brace and bit or whatever tool worked best, to put in the dynamite sticks. He would then light the fuses and try to crawl out in time. Sometimes there were cave-ins and other dangers, and he often came home injured. He couldn't afford a doctor, but fortunately, my Grandmother, Clara, had nurses training, and she would tend to his injuries and tape him up as best she could so he could return to work.

One time my Dad, Errol, went down the elevator shaft with Grandfather to watch him work. He never went back, saying that was enough for him. It was a terribly hard, dangerous life, but Dad said that was the best paying job Grandfather could get in the winters during the Depression. Life was indeed very harsh for some people back then.

Neighbors and Other Characters

6837A   Farm Festival, Rippey, Iowa

Farm Festival Rippey, Iowa Circa 1910

More Thoughts while drinking morning coffee and remembering . . . .
By Julene Ann Rittgers Boza

Mrs. Edith Crandell Church Youth Group would go caroling in the evenings at Christmas time and we would never miss Mrs. Crandell's home. You could smell her homemade cookies as you approached her porch. She always invited us into her kitchen for cookies and more songs. Cinnamon, ginger, chocolate – close your eyes and just go back to her kitchen.

Sandra Thornburgh and I have been friends since Kindergarten. Our dads drove school buses and operated the two restaurants/cafes in Rippey. Her family's home was above their cafe on Main Street and I lived in the old Hagerman home on Main Street. In the winter, Sandra and I would build very large snowmen/women in the vacant area of my home next to the highway – across the highway from the Ross Hatfield gas station and the railroad tracks.

In the summer months, Sandra and I would ride the train to Perry to see the movie. One of our parents would pick us up after the movie and drive back to Rippey.

We used to walk south down the railroad tracks to the bridge and just talk about teenage stuff. We walked many, many times but only once got caught by an oncoming northbound train. We scurried off the bridge in time, but what a surprise.

Special occasions at school with big potluck lunches and food items donated by parents were fun. I always volunteered my mother to bake her famous chocolate cake and make her great potato salad. One time, Sandra and I took Mother's two delicious items to school but could not find them when we went through the food line. Later, we found them, untouched, because they had been missed by the servers. We took them back to my home and ate large portions of chocolate cake and potato salad. Mother was disappointed because she had spent time and money in preparation, but she also knew the food would be enjoyed by her family. (I wonder if Sandra remembers this.)

There used to be band concerts in the town square. Some folks remember a wooden band stand which would be wheeled into the town square for the band members to sit on – I can't recall if I ever sat on this band stand – darn memory. I played clarinet and later bass clarinet in the band and Sandra played tenor sax. The two cafes (Rittgers and Thornburgh) took turns providing a free treat to the band members after the concerts.

Later in our teenage years, we had just begun dating two boys from Perry. Sandra wanted to switch dates and I liked both boys, so it did not matter to me. Next date, Sandra got in the front seat and I got in the back seat with our "new" dates. The boys laughed and all was o.k. Eventually, Sandra married her new date, Larry Huitt. The nice young man who had been my new date was killed in the Korean (I think) war.

I hope Larry and Sandra Huitt in Arizona read this part of my memory.

Jay and Winnie States Drug Store where I spent lots of time buying comic books and getting black and white film developed. Their drug store and Dad's restaurant shared a common wall.

Art Todd loved my mother's lemon pie. When I was a freshman (I think), **Mrs. Frame** was my Home Econ teacher. She helped all us girls plan an educational trip, which she would chaperone, and she encouraged us to hold fund raisers to pay for this trip. One popular fund raiser was to hold bake sales at **Roy Rains'** grocery store.

Girls baked and mothers baked – of course, I volunteered my mother to bake lemon pies. Art Todd was always there early and bought mother's lemon pie still warm from the oven. He was a regular customer.

Lulu Davis won a raffle, which was another fund raiser for our educational trip. We sold tickets and the winning ticket would get their car washed, polished, and detailed. Lulu lived just south of the Burk garage; she had a very old black car which had never been washed and the black paint had oxidized. It was in bad shape. Guess who won the raffle?? Yes, Lulu Davis! It took all of us girls all day to do her car but what a difference. Folks came from miles around just to admire Lulu's car. This was the last and only fund-raising car washing raffle we did.

And regarding the Educational Trip: We went to Denver and Rocky Mountain Park, chaperoned by **Mrs. Frame**, on a Greyhound bus, and thought it was great fun. "The times, they are a'changing. . ."

Hobos on the Perry Highway. When I was very young, my family lived on the Wesley Rittgers farm two miles south of town just off the Perry Highway (moved there when I was maybe 2, 1941-43). My dad was running the Home Café restaurant in town which left my mother and me alone a lot. Hobos on the highway would cut across the field and come to our home asking for food. Mother was always very afraid when they came. She would tell them her husband ran the Home Café in town and if they would go there, Wes would feed them. And Wes always did, plus usually let them sleep in the jail cell which was in the Fire Station building just north of the First National Bank.

I remember when Dad's restaurant burned. It was at night. At that time, we had left the farm and had built a home where Myron and Maralynn Rinker live now. Mother, little sister Marna, and I stood at the kitchen sink facing north watching the flames in the sky. We were two blocks south of the fire. The ceilings in the restaurant were a metal material which held the heat in. Dad had a tv set in the restaurant which melted. I had always thought dad owned the restaurant, but he did not. He made a trip to Nebraska to talk to the owner about rebuilding. When the restaurant was rebuilt, there was a pool hall in the back half of the building. Marna and I do not know who actually owned the restaurant, or when it sold and who purchased it. If anybody knows these answers, I would love to hear from you.

Grape Jelly. When we lived in the Hagerman home on Main Street, there was an open car port with grape vines all over it. One year, mother decided to make grape jelly. Bless her heart, it was such a job. Seeds and skins, etc; finally, boiling the juice and sugar which never, never thickened. Now that I have made jams and jellies, there is a product call Sure Jell which would have made the grape jelly thicken. Mother never tried to make grape anything after that experience.

I remember the old schoolhouse building near the highway. The school buses were parked in the basement. When winter weather came, my dad would be up early starting all the buses. My dad's Aunt Stellie Hunt Steward went to school in that building. My sister remembers her telling how she rode her horse to and from school.

Bob Ethel, school bus driver. When I began Kindergarten, I lived on the Rittgers farm. I did not want to go to school and cried every morning; daddy Wes carried me to the bus while my mother cried. The solution was my bus driver; he let me sit in the seat right behind him. When we got to railroad tracks, I was the one who got off the bus to check for trains and, if no trains, waved the bus across the tracks. Bob Ethel was my bus driver. I told my mother he had rusty teeth, a comment my mother enjoyed.

Charlie Wishman, School Custodian. I remember Charlie pushing us very young kids on his large wide mop as he cleaned the wide hallway on the first floor in the

Rippey School building. We would stand on the mop holding onto the handle, as Charlie pushed the mop down the long hallway.

My younger sister, Marna Kay Rittgers Parker. Sometime after 1957, the school system changed; Rippey and Grand Junction became East Greene and my sister (who lived in Rippey) rode the bus to Grand Junction for classes. Two towns who had been rivals in sports for umpteen years now were supposed to form teams. She was a very good basketball player; the team would practice and play games in East Greene; sometimes, they would practice in the large new gym at the Rippey School (the one which was being built when I graduated high school in 1957). Marna told me when she was a Junior (1963, the year Kennedy was assassinated), if the East Greene Girls Basketball Team could have won just one more game, they would have been in the "Sweet 16 Tournament." When both of us played basketball, girl teams played half-court; today, they play full court just like the boys. This is a Wonderment!

One more memory and I will stop for this time. Part of the top floor of the Rippey School building was the assembly for high schoolers; we were seated alphabetically by grade. For four years I sat between Philip Roberts and Ronnie Riley; i.e. Riley, Rittgers, Roberts. And for four years, those two male classmates smelled sooo good; I love Old Spice to this day and every time I smell it, I close my eyes and just go back.

LaVerne Groves
By Jerald Fessler through his son, Clark Fessler

Jerald Fessler of rural Rippey published his collections of stories, poetry, and remembrances in 2004, 17 years prior to his death.

At Mary Weaver's request, his son, Clark, shared the publication with her recently.

In writing his journal he reflects on people known within the community, as Jerald spent lots of time visiting with others at the local hangouts, Secress Café, or Sparky's. This excerpt is entitled LAVERNE GROVES:

Vern hired a man to help pick ear corn one fall. The man was also going to stay at Vern's house during the harvest. He was under a doctor's care with instructions to check his urine on a daily basis. He placed a coffee can under his bed for this purpose. Vern's brother-in-law, Guy Rice, was also working there. Guy was putting food coloring in the empty can, using a different color daily. I guess the fellow was just about driven nuts before they told him what was going on.

The Bench
By Marna Rittgers Parker

During my early years, I lived with my sister and parents in what we called the Hagerman House. It's still there on the main street of Rippey. The brick two-story house at the end of the street – three stories if you count the attic! Next door was the Home Cafe, the restaurant and pool hall my dad Wesley operated with the help of my mother Mae. There was a long wooden bench outside the building that became the favorite spot for the town's older gentlemen to gather, visit, exchange stories, and gossip. Some of these fellows I still remember.

Chester A. Stroud, known to everyone as "Chet," was a World War I Navy veteran. He always wore "bibby" overalls. Chet like to whittle while sitting on that bench. I can remember watching him as he crafted different things from sticks of wood. If I brought him "just the right stick," he would whittle something for me. I can still see his well-worn hands with that little pocketknife he used. How I wish that now I'm a lot older I could visit with him and ask questions about his experiences in the war and afterwards. But since I was so young and stupid, I didn't think about that. Just wanted to see what Chet would make for me out of "just the right stick."

Another one of the regulars on the bench was **Harold "Sparry" McCain**. He lived on a piece of property on the other side of the railroad tracks. He had chickens, milk cows, and did some farming. Sparry walked with a noticeable limp. The best thing I remember about Mr. McCain – he had a team of horses! I loved horses and always wanted one of my very own. That dream came true when I married John Parker. His father Jack gave to me my very own horse. Mr. McCain loved to show his team. He would hitch them up to a small wagon and drive them uptown. I was in heaven! He would even let me pet them. I remember one day I was playing outside. There was an alley that ran behind the Hagerman House. I heard a commotion – the rattling of snaps and chains. And there in the alley was Mr. McCain and his team. He had stopped and waited for me to get through the fence and to the alley, so I could see the horses up close and personal. Oh, wow! How special was that! Sparry was a gentle and kind man, and you could tell he loved those two horses.

Occasionally a gentleman by the name of **Axel Berglund** would make it to the bench. With brain power assistance from the Bardole sisters, Nancy Hanaman and Sharon McBlain, I was able to fill in the blank spots of my memory about Axel. Mr. Berglund had been the station master at the Rippey train depot. That's when trains actually stopped in Rippey! He had a physical disability, so he walked with a cane. It would take him awhile, but he would eventually make it to the bench. He wouldn't stay long because it was going to take him a good while to make it back home. As a young girl walking home from school, I would see Axel many times standing in front of his house in the afternoons. I would always greet him; he would smile and wave. I think he waited for the school kids to walk by his house just so he could see us. I don't know much about him other than what Nancy and Sharon told me, but I do remember that very nice and gentle man waiting on the sidewalk in front his house for the children to walk by in the afternoons.

Other bench sitters were **Ralph Johnson** and **Ernie Clapp**. The story goes that Ernie was a farrier and while shoeing a horse got kicked in the back of his head. As a result he had a very large lump that formed. He lived with this the rest of his life. I always wondered what medical science could have done for him. I'm guessing Ernie never even bothered going to see a doctor.

The bench sitters. I've forgotten many of them. Wouldn't it be wonderful if in these days of technology, we would take the time to sit on a bench with our fellow man to visit, exchange information, and just be with one another?

Sitting still captures a moment that will be forever remembered

Summers of Bygone Days

An Element of the Mural Painted in Rippey, Iowa
By Sarah Stotts   Summer 2020

Summer in Rippey
By Mary Fry Liebich

When I was in high school, I ran a summer program for the city at the skating rink every weekday afternoon. We would skate, of course, and have organized games. We had arts and crafts, and competitions. Students would get the ribbons they'd won at a ceremony at the end of the summer. I remember Dan Brubaker and siblings being dropped off every day by his parents. Dan was probably five or six. And to this day when I see Dan, which is almost every day, I think of him coming those summers when he was a tiny guy compared to the town mayor he is now.

Speaking of the park, we had a horse show every summer, organized by I. J. Burk and Pink Grow and some others. It was in the area between the bleachers along the third base line and the cornfield at the ballpark. It was well attended.

They had a competition that called for each rider to do whatever the announcer said, immediately. When a rider made a mistake, that person was out. Well, it got down to me and Ginger and one other rider – I have no idea who. By the way, Ginger worked off of voice commands, so did what the announcer asked immediately. Finally, we were asked to dismount, which I did. And then get on again. Well, I couldn't get on from the ground. So, I led Ginger out of the arena and onto the baseball field to the pitcher's mound which was high enough that I could get on there. And I won!

Reflections About Rippey's Library
By Toni Averill Roberts

The Rippey Library, like the town itself, has changed a lot in the last twenty years. With the loss of many rural farms, circulation was drastically reduced. By 2005 the younger generation still participated in the Summer Reading programs but were much more interested in playing games on the computer or watching TV or movies instead of reading!

To accommodate those interests, the Rippey Library installed three computers for public use. Friends of Rippey, and the Bill Gates Foundation, helped with the funding of these computers. The State Library Association helped each library with funding and classes to set up their own WEB page to help inform the public of all the libraries' activities.

Many adults participated in a semi-annual book discussion in conjunction with the Greene County Library Association. Other programs offered included: travelogues (given by locals about trips abroad), a book signing by a former resident, and a photography show (by a renowned photography judge who was a hometown boy). An annual soup contest was held in January, a fun event to raise money and get people out and about during the doldrums of winter.

Besides using free Wi-Fi services, members of the community could also use the printer, fax, and copier for a nominal fee. The small community room in back was used by several local groups to play cards, hold meetings, and watch movies at special holidays. Every May the Rippey Alumni would meet for a reception and a chance to chat with classmates and view the Rippey High School class photos that adorned the walls.

By 2012 the library was "bursting at the seams" and needed a larger area to accommodate the collection and have more space for activities. Over the July 4th weekend the entire library was moved to the newly renovated building that had been the Masonic Hall. The momentous event was accomplished by the efforts of many volunteers, both adults and youngsters, and by financial help from the Friends of Rippey. In addition to a beautiful, spacious area for the library, there was also room for an upgraded kitchen area, bathrooms, and a large community room.

Everything was new—more computers, handsome wooden shelving, desk and counter space, and furniture to relax in while reading a book. After much sorting and weeding, the remaining collection was entered into the digital system using Dewey Decimal coding, and a scanner was added to check out material more efficiently.

Even though the role of the library has changed through the years "Libraries still remain the Heart" of their communities!

Rippey Library

Rippey Skating Rink
By Cindy Anderson Cole

I have enjoyed reading various memories from former Rippey residents. I grew up in Rippey and share many of the same memories; one of which was spending lots of time at the Rippey Skating Rink.

It was a big deal to go skating with all my friends and to buy treats from the concession stand. On one particular evening, I went to the stand to buy an orange soda and while I was standing there, another skater came in a little too fast and bumped me. (I remember who it was but won't mention his name.) I went down. The bottle came with me, broke and glass impaled into my hand. Someone drove me home with my hand bleeding. When my mom saw it, she almost fainted.

Dad drove me to Grand Junction to see Dr. Wetrich. He cleaned out all the glass and stitched me up with 14 purple stitches!!! I still have the scar. Anyway, I went back to the skating rink with my hand swollen and wrapped but it didn't stop me from skating!

Does anyone remember who was in charge of the music being played at the rink? They had some great tunes!

We had open skating, girls only, boys only, and couples skate. If I remember correctly. I always looked forward to couples skating because Denny Nail (who just recently passed away, what a great friend) and I had a great time skating. He taught me how to skate backwards!!!

I don't know what year they stopped having those official skate nights, but it was a wonderful thing for all of us Rippey kids. When I go back home, I always drive past the rink and smile.

Lucky to be from Rippey
By Fred Grow

I think back at how fortunate I was to grow up in Rippey. I was lucky to have a lot of family born and raised in Rippey, who lived there their whole lives and were a big part of the community. Like many other small towns back then, Rippey was a "community involved" town. During my childhood and teenage years, numerous little memories come to mind.

Baseball was a big part of the community. A large, white, square sign was put in the middle of Main Street letting everyone know there was a home game that night. There were Wednesday night band concerts in the middle of the downtown during the summer. On Tuesday and Friday nights, we went roller skating at the outdoor skating rink. Saturday afternoons during Thanksgiving and Christmas times, everyone came to town for the turkey drawings. Farm Union dances were held at the Rebekah Hall one Saturday night a month.

I grew up on a farm just east of Rippey. At the age of five I got my first pony, and I always had a riding horse of some kind for the remainder of my days living on the farm. At that time, you couldn't imagine how many town and country people alike had riding horses. One of my fondest memories was when all the people in Rippey with horses would meet most Sunday afternoons at I.J. Burk's horse barn and trail ride to Squirrel Hollow. We would have a potluck meal or a hot dog roast, and then ride back to Rippey together.

What a fun time. I am so glad to have had Rippey in my background.

Holidays

Halloween postcard from 1914

Easter Bunny Visits Kindergarten Class at Rippey School
By Marna Rittgers Parker

Let's see.... I can't remember exactly what year that Rabbit showed up – maybe 1951-52. I was in Maxine Johnson's kindergarten class. It was spring – almost Easter. We had been outside for recess. When our class got back to the classroom, what do our shining eyes see?! Footprints! Footprints all over the floor. They were big and white. Miss Johnson said they looked like rabbit tracks. What?! No way!

But as we looked at them, sure enough they looked like rabbit tracks. And there was candy! Candy – for the children! How did that rabbit get into the classroom? Footprints led to an open window! While we were outside, somehow, some way that Rabbit came in through the window, scampered around the classroom leaving candy, and exited the way he/she came in. Wow! We couldn't wait until we got home to tell our parents that the Easter Bunny came early to our school!

As I got older, I later surmised that this had been a set-up by Miss Johnson, our beloved teacher, and Charlie Wishman, the school custodian. The white footprints were most likely chalk dust. What was used to make the footprints, I can't say. All I know is this was one of best days in kindergarten.

Another story about Charlie Wishman. He always kept track of birthdays. If it was your birthday day, Mr. Wishman would pay you a visit and give you a birthday "horse bite" on your knee! How did he know it was your birthday day? Probably because you were wearing a crown that Miss Johnson had made especially for you. You got to tell her your favorite colors and she would fashion a crown from construction paper. You got to wear the crown all day. And later in the afternoon, your mother would show up with treats for the class!

Those, my friends, were just some of the grand days of growing up at Rippey School.

Memory of Rippey Fireworks

By Marna Rittgers Parker with help from her sister, Julene Rittgers Hunt   June 11, 2015

It all started in the late 1940's or early 1950's. Our father, Wesley Daniel Rittgers, had a farm outside Rippey off the highway to Perry. I believe that farm is now owned by the Brown family but I could be wrong. Our uncle Kenneth "Stix" Riley (married to our mother's sister Bernie) was a trucker. Julene remembers it was a refrigerated truck carrying cheese and butter. It was illegal for an individual to purchase fireworks in Iowa so Uncle Stix would stop in a state that did have fireworks during his travels. Wesley and Stix would set the fireworks off in the front yard of the farmhouse. Julene remembers that. Me? I was a baby and only cared about food and clean diapers. Folks in Rippey could see the fireworks from the town and a few ventured out to the farm to watch. As a result of its popularity, Stix would bring back more fireworks every year. At some point in time – neither Julene nor I know exactly when – town fathers asked Wesley and Stix to bring the fireworks to town so more people could enjoy them. It was then that the town began purchasing the fireworks for them to use. Evidently a town or city could purchase fireworks in Iowa but not an individual.

Wesley and Stix were glad to oblige. And so began the tradition of fireworks in Rippey after the baseball game. They were set off on the other side of the outfield fence. When I was older, I can remember Wesley readying the "launch pads" for the mortars. He would take a five gallon bucket, put a piece of heavy duty pipe in the bucket and fill the bucket up with sand. Today, most of the displays are controlled by computers. Back then it was Wesley and Stix setting them off with flares. It's a wonder they didn't blow themselves up!

During the years different helpers volunteered. I hate to admit I can only remember two – Merle "Zip" Coon and by then brother-in-law Rod Hunt. Great story about the year Rod helped Wesley. Rod and Julene were living in Chicago at the time and came to Rippey for the Fourth. Uncle Stix was having health issues then – he was still recuperating from his first heart attack. Rod volunteered to help. He hadn't planned on an adventure like this so didn't have any old clothes with him. You had to wear something old because burn holes would ruin your clothes – particularly your pants. Well Grandpa Charlie had a pair of old pants that Rod could squeeze into. Everything was going well until one of the mortars misfired. Instead of zooming up, it went up a few feet and made a turn right towards Wesley and Rod! Fortunately, the town had built a bathroom by the skating rink. Both Wesley and Rod ran to the ladies facility and slammed the door just at the rocket went off! Boom! Different color sparks were everywhere! There was a lull; the crowd was quiet; no one knew if they had been injured or what had happened. Shortly, the door of the bathroom opened up and we could hear those two laughing like two hyenas! Rod would tell that story for years to come.

When Zip helped with the fireworks, it was hard for the crowd to tell Wesley apart from Zip. For you long-time Rippey residents, you will remember that both Wes and Zip almost always wore bibby overalls with white t-shirts, and both were big men! In the distance from the bleachers, you could see two figures out in center field dressed alike. Never could tell which one was Wes and which one was Zip!

Neither Julene nor I can remember what year Rippey stopped having a fireworks display on the Fourth. For years it was tradition – baseball, hot dogs and cold drinks from the concession stand, band concert, and fireworks! I will never forget those years. Nor will I forget how the whole thing started – a family getting together at the farm on the Fourth with fireworks by Wes and Stix!

I Remember Rippey
By Kathy Lansman Young

I attended school in Rippey from 1st grade (Evelyn Wilson) through 8th grade when we consolidated with Grand Junction and became East Greene.

Some of my favorite memories revolve around Halloween, dressing up and meeting at the Rebekah Hall where we would go in groups to collect money for UNICEF, then come back to the Hall for a party. When parents showed up to pick us up, they had to be careful to get into town and back out again before the high school kids ~ and sometimes Sheriff Riley ~ would block off all the streets into and out of town, collect an outhouse or two and make a pile of lumber and tires in the middle of town with the outhouses on top. I remember one Halloween when they turned Burks' horses loose.

I remember the skating at the roller rink ~ I'm not sure which night it was held during the summer, but a lot of us kids showed up to skate to the music. Norman Devilbiss could really skate, and we all wanted to emulate him!

Halloween Memories
By Ellen Johnston

Fall work for farmers was often still in progress, so Grandma Lila would come to pass out treats, while my mom, Janice Johnston, would take my brother and me out trick or treating around the Rippey neighborhood. Dressed in costumes, my most memorable outfit was a soapbox topped with balloon bubbles. Some notable houses we stopped at include the man with the cherry tree who passed out turnips as treats. Maxine Johnson passed out full-sized candy bars. Walt and Nadine Anderson gave us individual treat bags. Somebody passed out red popcorn balls, but I can't recall who, while a man down at the senior home would give each visitor a quarter. One year it snowed, so we drove as far as Harvey and Joyce Rice's house. Decorations were seen on homes around town–corn husks, and pumpkins in the yard, as well as orange garbage bags filled with leaves. The Rippey Methodist Church cleaned pumpkins, and one year we remember members wore the empty shells as masks.

Photo: This knight in shining armor is Harrison Johnson in 2016.

Rippey Methodist Church Annual Halloween Costume Party
By Mike Scharingson

It was the fall of 1959 and I was in the 3rd grade, I being Mike Scharingson, and in desperate need of a costume idea. At that time my grandma on my father's side, Maude Egan, was living with us. She was a small little lady, in fact about my size. I do not remember if she or my mother, Dorothy Dorris Scharingson, came up with the costume idea. It was decided I should go as a lady wearing my grandmother's clothes and the mask of young lady.

I, of course, thought it was a poor idea, but my opinion was not important. The night arrived and each costume was judged and, lo and behold, I came in 2nd place, but this is where the story gets interesting. The judge was Margaret Dorris, my aunt, who had no idea that she had just awarded 2nd place to her nephew. When I lifted my mask and she saw it was me, she was mortified. Everyone else thought it was hilarious and I was just happy I won.

Mike Scharingson dressed for Halloween 1959

Halloween
By Mary Fry Liebich

The little kids would do their trick or treat thing. Then we would go up to Main Street to see what the bigger boys were up to. Rol (pronounced Raul) – Roland Riley, the town marshal, would rope off Main Street. The older boys would bring all sorts of stuff and dump it on Main Street. Then the adults as well as the kids would come to see what "decorated" Main Street. At a certain point they would have to put it all back where it came from.

I remember an outhouse sitting at the top of the hill – in the street south of the telephone office. And an old bathtub and whatever else they'd been mentally collecting until Halloween came.

Halloween
By Nancy Bardole Hanaman

I remember Halloween when we young kids walked from house to house in Rippey trick or treating and gathered many tasty treats. These included the popcorn that my Grandmother Alberta Bardole prepared to our delight each year. Later in the evening, the high school kids, mostly boys, I think, would build brick barricades in some of the dimly lighted streets and an outhouse would find a new home on Main Street much to the displeasure of Rippey residents. No harm done but a bit inconvenient.

That Frankenstein Mask!!
By Steve Nail

As I recall, it was a Saturday morning, just prior to Halloween; the year was 1969. I had just purchased a Frankenstein mask preparing for that event and wanted to show this very realistic looking find to my friends at the First National Bank in Rippey.

I had known Clark, Myron, and Maybelle for years and had stopped in just to say hello, with or without a deposit or in need of a loan. This trio was just a fun group to be around. So, with that as a relationship backdrop, the thought of placing that full head cover mask over my head and walking into that bank and expecting anything but a compliment on how realistic it looked didn't really cross my mind. **WRONG!**

As I climbed the bank stairs, threw open the door and entered the lobby four feet from the counter, I quickly realized that my idea was not impressing anyone and could have been correctly identified as a felony in a court of law. Luckily there were no customers in the bank at the time to witness this very awkward situation.

Clark was in his office, Myron and Maybelle were behind the counter and I quickly realized that none of them knew it was me under that mask and what was to happen next. At this point, neither did I. After what seemed like minutes had passed without conversation, I finally began to figure out the reality of the situation. The look on the faces of Myron and Maybelle will remain with me forever. I decided to identify myself, pulled off the mask and witnessed the sigh of relief combining with the elevating notice of anger at the same time. As we finally started to engage in limited conversation and color began to return to the faces of those three bank employees, the atmosphere began to lighten and the belief that my original intention of making their day with a little humor was gradually being accepted.

Luckily, at this point there were still no additional patrons who had entered the bank. After apologizing and promising that I would never, ever, ever pull that one again, I left the bank. This crazy event was asked about for days, weeks and months and I still get asked about it to this day. I doubt I made their day, but I do know that I created a memory. Only in small town Iowa could someone pull this off and still be friends with those you placed at the risk of cardiac arrest, and then turn around the next day and be approved for a loan at a fair and unbiased rate!

Thanks to Rippey, the First National Bank, especially Myron Rinker, and the late Clark Bardole and Maybelle Wisecup. What an understanding group who witnessed and recovered that day, or maybe the day after, from this once in a 150-year event

Poppies
By Mary Fry Liebich`

I remember selling poppies and being able to go into the saloon at the end of Main Street—just north of where the car wash is now and a bit east of where the post office is now. This was the only time that kids were allowed in there and the folks there did buy the poppies.

A Christmas Story
By Marna Rittgers Parker

Right after Thanksgiving, the merchants in Rippey sponsored a Saturday giveaway on Main Street – Burk's Garage, First National Bank, Killam's Hardware Store, and Clover Leaf Grocery Store were located at the intersection where the drawing was held. As you shopped in the stores during the week, you filled out a card and that ended up in a hopper for Saturday's drawing. I remember I won a frozen turkey!

The Saturday before Christmas was for the kids – Santa would come to town. I was older but we still lived in the Hagerman House. My dad Wesley came in with a box and in that box was a Santa suit. He had been asked to play Santa for the Saturday drawing. My dad was a big guy and the Santa suit didn't really fit him, but it was the only one available so he had to wear it. And the beard – white cotton beard – didn't cover up his face very well.

Kids didn't care – it was Santa and he was passing out bags of candy, peanuts, and fruit. Wesley had been working for the school district as a custodian and bus driver. As a result, he knew all the local kids. Can you imagine the joy they felt when Santa handed them their bag of goodies calling them by name! Not like your usual mall Santa. This Santa actually knew their names! If some of the kids recognized him behind his ill-fitting beard, they didn't say. They were happy to get a bag of goodies compliments of the Rippey merchants.

Christmas Caroling
By Marna Rittgers Parker

Pearl Chase had our route all planned out. Walking around in the cold and snow to sing to the older residents of the town. What a wonderful way to celebrate Christmas.

Methodist Church Rippey, Iowa

Rippey Today

Fire Chief Peter Johnson with new helmets 2018

Rippey Fire Station

2020 Bike Ride to Rippey
By Mary Dorris Weaver

Rippey welcomed the 43rd BRR (Bike Ride to Rippey) event on Saturday February 1, 2020. Always weather dependent, the ride has seen as many as 2,000 riders dressed in winter biking garb or outlandish crazy costumes.

Started in 1976 by Jim Walstrom and Dennis Hurley of Perry to escape their winter cabin fever, BRR remains the first ride of the year, being held the first Saturday of February. The ride was developed as a method to beat the winter blahs and to refute the attitude that nothing happens in Iowa during the winter. The first year, 10 riders ventured out from Perry to Rippey, Iowa, a round trip of 24 miles. The BRR ride has morphed into a major fund raising event for the Perry Chamber and several organizations in Rippey.

For 2020 Rippey brought out the Welcome Mat for these hardy souls by offering beverages, including adult beverages, roast beef sundaes, a baked potato bar, and tempting sweets to replenish the calories burned on that northwest 12 mile trip. Non-biker gawkers were also welcomed to partake in the food and observe the frivolity.

The Thirsty Pig, under contract with the Friends of Rippey, sold beer, shots, and soft drinks on the Main Street of the town. Profits were shared and added to the Rippey Sesquicentennial fund.

The Rippey United Methodist Church provided their traditional baked potato bar with a plethora of toppings–broccoli, cheese, butter, sour cream, and chili. Pies and bars were served along with hot chocolate, coffee, and water to provide energy and as a warm up for the return trip to Perry.

The Rippey Lion's Club served their usual Roast Beef Sundaes at the Community Center. For those who question this Rippey delight, it is ROBUST. It begins with mashed potatoes, a tender slice of roast beef that is then smothered with beef gravy, all served in a bowl topped with a cherry tomato. This is a must for first time riders. The Lions also had chili and bars, along with water, coffee, and hot chocolate.

BRR is a big fund raiser for the Lion's Club, as they use the dollars to provide Christmas gifts, contribute to Camp Hertko, and aid with numerous other Rippey community activities.

The photo opportunity sponsored by the Friends of Rippey as a fundraiser for the Sesquicentennial.... "I froze my _ss on the BRR ride" was popular for Facebook posts. (See photo below.) Donations were added for the upcoming community celebration.

All riders were encouraged to leave Rippey by 4:00 P.M. on the paved county road E57 and south to P54 at Berkley to State Highway 144 Diagonal back to Perry.

Fourteen portable toilets courtesy of the City of Rippey were positioned around the town for the guests.

Photo Opportunity

2020. East of Rippey. Going by the barn quilts on the property of Doris Stewart. Photograph by Des Moines Register. Used by Permission

Rippey Wind Farm
By Mary Dorris Weaver

The flatness of the prairie landscape changed to the north and west of Rippey in 2012. Twenty wind turbine generators were erected about 3 miles north, in an east to west arc of about 10 miles between Rippey and Grand Junction. During the summer of 2012 almost 100 workers erected the 328 feet high turbines.

During a personal visit to the construction with friends during that summer, the late LaVerne Erickson, land owner of a turbine site, was on the job completing his "daily inspection". He, like many others, was excited to see the landscape "begin to bloom with these regal towers."

Another highlight of our visit to the site, was to observe the entrepreneurial efforts of some of the neighborhood children who made food available to the workers. The menu included popcorn, cinnamon rolls, hamburgers, and pulled pork sandwiches. Their mom later informed me they made enough money to purchase all of their school clothes.

Many summer evenings this writer was able to observe the turbine work area ablaze with lights, as the lifting and placement of the blades was more easily done at night when the wind was minimal.

 Here are some additional facts for those who are interested:

The blade length was 164 feet, so ground to tip of blade is 492 feet at the high point. The blade weighs 10.8 tons, and the tower is held in position by 730.6 yards of concrete. To continue to review the structure, the small building at the top is called a "nacelle" or referred to as the doghouse. It is about the size of a public transportation bus. It contains the generator, the brakes, and the yaw. It converts the wind (kinetic energy) into electricity.

The contracting company was RPM (Renewable Power Market) Access. Twenty-eight landowners and 3,500 acres comprise the wind farm; 3.6 miles of access roads were built to the turbines; and almost ten miles of underground wiring collection was completed, but all with efficiency as only 20 farmable acres became non-tillable.

The blades were delivered by escort semi-truck in May of 2012, after being manufactured in Arkansas. A mere breeze of 6.71 miles per hour will cause electricity to be created, but if the wind reaches higher than 56 miles per hour, the computer associated with the turbine will shut it down. A final wind speed fact: the tip speed of the blade will travel up to 172.2 miles per hour.

The electricity generated is being sold to Central Iowa Power Cooperative under a 25 year contract agreement. The $75 million investment from Google, their second wind energy investment, will produce electricity for up to 15,000 homes.

RPM continues to be a good neighbor as they provide philanthropic donations to Rippey as well as other Greene County projects.

The photo shows the "signing" of a blade by the landowners and neighbors. The RPM Company and the Rippey coordinator, Jim Diamond, were good neighbors, hosting several meals as information was shared with the land owners. Specific information for this article was provided by him. Rippeyites hold fond remembrances of him, as he maintained his office in a corner of the Rippey Library Community Room.

Notes

Rippey Always in My Heart

Memorial to Rippey Consolidated School

Happy Birthday, Rippey.
I'm proud to call you my hometown.
By Mary Fry Liebich

Let's see....

I remember being a member of the Rippey band—played baritone with Sharon Bardole, Phil Roberts, and Bill Souder—and playing in the town square once a week during the summer. Then the band members were treated to something at the Thornburg café--a drink, an ice cream cone, or whatever—afterwards.

The marching band would practice at the baseball park. Well, the outfield where we marched was full of garter snakes, and we were supposed to stay in straight lines. Besides, if you were playing a baritone, it was hard to see the ground to see where the snakes were. Not fun!

Mom was the postmaster for several years when I was a kid. The Rippey Post Office was in the back of the First National Bank building. Mom had hung up a Rippey Savings Bank calendar and a First National Bank calendar in the open part of the post office—where people came to open their post office boxes and get their mail. Well, the official post office inspectors (state, I suppose) came and said "Nope, no advertising." So, Mom cut off the part at the bottom of the calendars that had the names of the banks and left the calendars up. Of course, everyone knew which was from which bank.

I would get home from school, put something in the oven for supper, and climb on Ginger, my horse. Sometimes I'd put on the saddle and martingale and bridle; sometimes I'd just put on a halter and rope and we'd go around town with Patches, the dog.

By the time I was in 7th grade, Ginger and another horse, were staked out along the road for grass during the day.

Even though students weren't supposed to go off the school grounds during the day, I was allowed to go to the horses and move them during the noon hour. Often that was north of the house between us and Denekas and sometimes up by Ernie Clapp's barn and sometimes the grass between Jake Peter's house and the baseball park.

If a player hit a foul ball that went out of the baseball park past the third base line or past the first base line into where the cars were parked, the kids would get it and take it to the announcer, who would give them 5 cents for bringing it back. The little slot they put the return ball into so that the umpire could pick it up is still there in the stadium. Bring in a couple of foul balls and you'd have enough money to get something from the food stand.

My Love for Rippey
By Clark Fessler

Rippey had a huge influence on the person I am and the direction I took in life. Growing up close enough to see the lights of the ballpark glowing over the horizon. Dreaming of being a ball player. And the day I could play on that magnificent diamond. (That at that time looked like Yankee Stadium to me.) While my address was RR#1 Perry. I always claimed Rippey as home. It is where I enjoyed my first lemon coke with my grandfather, watched countless card games and absorbed the personalities and humor that made this town.

Growing up a farm boy, the center of my world was Rippey and those that called it home. Two banks (the one you talked out loud and the one you whispered), two car dealers (those cool director chairs with car names), two service stations (the adventures of getting a tire fixed at Ross Hatfield's Coop station), the school where I started my education and my parents finished theirs, and the ball park. What more could you need?

From the beginning I loved this farming community and its unique ability when help was needed to drop all differences and personal animosities to rally to whatever cause was necessary to get someone else's life back on track. Spending my teenage years baling hay, shelling corn, and walking so many rows of beans I still can see them when I close my eyes taught me the value of a job well done. As I neared graduation from high school and the reality that I was not the next Mickey Mantle set in (nor was I the next Lester Zanotti or Danny Peters.), I turned to the second love, farming. My teacher advisors were devastated to the point they called me into the guidance office to talk me out of "wasting my life" farming.

Being third generation stubborn, I decided to show them! For the next 35 years I thoroughly loved wasting my life! More than the job, I loved the camaraderie that went with the life and the extra special way it felt in the Rippey community. I learned great life lessons from the outstanding characters of this community as a boy, a teenager, and a man. The list of people from Rippey that made these years great is quite long. As the story goes: "They just don't make them like that anymore!" And that is how I will always feel about Rippey! Thank you for the memories! Happy 150 years!

Memories of Rippey 1943 – 1961
By Sharon Bardole McBlain

My graduating class of 1961 had twelve members. Six of my fellow classmates married each other and ended up farming near Rippey. I headed off to Simpson College, and Rippey became the place which always lives in my heart but never again was where I lived.

I grew up on a farm. When I was small, we had an outhouse and no indoor plumbing. We had electricity but kept kerosene lamps handy for the frequent loss of power. We still had a coal house. Mom burned corn cobs in the cast iron stove in the kitchen. The house was heated with a coal burning stove in the dining room. The upstairs was unheated. I slept with my little sister Nancy. Her back was great for warming cold feet.

Dad worked in the town at the First National Bank. He also always had large vegetable and flower gardens. He raised some farm animals for family food. My childhood was not filled with the chores and hard work of most of my rural classmates.

In my memory, my brother John, sister Nancy and I filled our days with fun things such as baseball, climbing trees, target practice using tin cans, playing with kittens, lying on our backs and watching the clouds, and occasionally finding some rotten eggs and throwing them at the side of the coal house. In the evenings, we played caroms, Authors, Flinch and other card and board games. Mom always read to us at night and made sure we had books to read. I could never understand why her voice would often slow down and then come to a halt as she began to drift off to sleep in the middle of the story.

We farm children lived mostly within the confines of the family unit. Our playmates were our siblings with most of our interaction with other children at school or at church. We were lucky because similarly aged cousins lived just a quarter of a mile up the road and the Heater family was just a half mile in another direction. It always seemed to me that the "sophisticated" town kids must be having more fun. They were able to meet up with playmates and freely roam around town playing chalk the corner, hide and seek and other games. They had paved streets to ride their bikes on, sidewalks to roller skate on, a hill to slide down in the winter and could easily get together. They also had lots of nearby houses to Trick or Treat on Halloween!

Our breakfast was almost always milk, eggs, bacon, and toast with jam. We would jump up from the table, brush our teeth and rush to catch the bus that often was already stopped at the end of our driveway. Irwin Corey, the driver, always gave us a welcoming smile.

Kindergarten through 5th grade was on the first floor of the Rippey school and 6th through 12th on the second. Recess was often roller skating on the circle driveway, playing German bat ball on the small diamond, or playing on the playground equipment. We were warned not to go into the row of pine trees along the back edge of the playground.

Rippey was proud of its hot lunch program run by local ladies. I still remember the local women who cooked and served our food. We filed through the line and carried our food back to our classroom where we sat at our desks to eat. You had to eat ALL of your food before you could head out to recess. I have fond memories of Ethel Correy serving our food and Charlie Wishman, our much-loved school custodian.

The Rippey community gathered in the tiny, old gray gym to watch high school basketball games in the winter. I became a member of the rousing Rippey Pep Band in the 4th grade. We played the National Anthem and various college fight songs during the games. Some of us didn't always hit all of the right notes, but we were enthusiastic and we were loud! I have fond memories of class plays and band concerts on the stage in that little gym. I also have fond memories of the programs of Al Bell, who came from time to time and presented exciting talks about his travels to interesting places.

I remember that our 7th grade basketball games were held in that small gym but am not sure about the 8th grade games. I feel sure that our 9th grade games were played in the wonderful new gym.

Rippey had its own phone company until for a while after I graduated from high school. A large crank phone hung on the wall in our dining room. Our phone number was 23 on 75. A very long, continuous ring meant that it was an important announcement for everyone. Sometimes it was to report that a town team baseball game had been canceled or postponed or to give updated information on the fireworks. The long ring was also used to let us know school was being called off due to weather or impassable roads. The woman who sat at the switch board in the telephone office did not appreciate it when high school kids wanted to make calls after 10 at night.

Rippey High School merged with East Greene two years before I graduated. And now the town of Rippey is about to celebrate 150 years. Thanks to all of you who are working on this celebration.

Positively Memorable
By John Rains

It was the 31st of December 1959, and the Rains Family–
Roy, Evelyn, Bob, John, and Jerry–arrived in Rippey,
moving from a farm 6 miles south of Glidden, IA. Mom and
Dad had bought the "Clover Farm" grocery store from the
Saiters. This was a big move for the Rainses, after living
on a farm for all our lives. I had just turned 14 a month
earlier. On the farm there was something going on all the
time and in town, not so much, other than working in my
folks' store. As time went on, working in the store wasn't
so bad, especially after Dad started teaching me how to cut
meat. That became my duty on Saturdays when I wasn't
working on the farm.

New Year's Day, 1960, was spent taking inventory of the
contents of the store. Have you ever counted Kool-Aid
packets, potatoes, and many other little things of mind-
boggling numbness? Not fun! I longed to be outside
driving a tractor! Once summer came I started working for
various farmers, which made life more bearable. The pay
was $1.00 an hour, regardless of what I was doing, from
driving a tractor to cleaning out hog houses. I loved
working on the farm, regardless of my assigned tasks.
Average income at this time was $4,000-$5,000 per year.
The second spring I started working for Chuck and Ruth
Newhouse and worked for them the remainder of high
school. My last day working for Chuck was the day before I
left for Army basic training, June 14th, 1964.

The year before, I had joined the Army National Guard,
June 13th, 1963, at the encouragement (talked into it) by
Fred Grow. Fred and I joined on the "Buddy Plan" which
lasted until we arrived at Ft. Leonard Wood, Missouri. On
the second day there we were separated due to my
enlistment physical being 366 days old, so I had to have a

new physical exam. Fred's enlistment date was a week behind mine since his physical exam was delayed for a week from mine. Oh well, we both survived the rigors of basic training!

One of the things anyone dreads when they move during junior high/high school is making friends and wondering if you will be accepted in the new school. I was well received and accepted in the eighth grade class! Other than the first day, I don't remember any frustration of not being accepted. High school was a lot of fun and many, many memories were created. Extracurricular activities were many – basketball, track, football (Senior year, 1st year for EG), chorus, band, small groups for chorus. My football career was pretty short, 2 ¼ games, because a kid from Ballard Huxley laid my nose over on my right cheek bone!

I could go on with many stories, but that would be boring. My years in Rippey were positively memorable. The class of 1964 was a good class and still has a great time of being together.

Random Memories of Growing Up in Rippey
By Marna Rittgers Parker

Winters were great for kids—not so much for the parents. Snow forts, snowball fights, fox and goose, snow angels. All great games. I will never forget sledding down the long hill at the Scharingson farm outside of Rippey. Beware of the big fire roaring at the bottom of the hill. Hot chocolate served to all sledders and dish riders by the host family.

Halloween nights in Rippey. Getting all dressed up in our costumes and heading out. No worries about bad things happening to you, though there was usually at least one parent along. The best part—homemade treats. Cookies, fudge, caramels, popcorn balls—all made especially for Halloween trick or treaters. Back in those days, no one even thought about putting something dangerous in the goodies.

The night the grain elevator burned. Mother woke me up so I could see what was happening. Wesley was, of course, at the site doing what little could be done with one Rippey fire truck. Other towns sent their trucks and volunteers. There was so much debris flying around in the air, it looked like Armageddon.

The night a call came into our house from someone in Dawson. There was a big fire in that town. Wesley and others in Rippey rallied to help. Problem was there was a huge blizzard at the time. A snowplow headed up the caravan, followed by a school bus with volunteers, and the Rippey fire truck brought up the rear. Some hours later, Wesley came in cold and tired. The Rippey team made it as far as the bridge over the Raccoon River and had to turn around. Even the snowplow couldn't get through. We found out later that trucks from Perry managed to get to Dawson to assist.

Basketball. Girls basketball. Played with six team members—three guards and three forwards divided by the center line. I have to say, the way girls' basketball is played these days just doesn't seem right. I know—I'm old.

Baseball—both town team and school kids. Seemed like there was always something going on at the ballpark.

Hayrides. Boy, kids these days don't know what they are missing out on not having hayrides.

The best memories of all are the wonderful people that lived in that little town—some are still there. Starting kindergarten with a group of kids and most of us ending up graduating from high school together along with some new additions. Connections and friendships that have lasted all these years.

Rippey Cemetery
By Marna Rittgers Parker

The Rippey Cemetery is the final resting place for so many of my family members. When Mother was still alive and my sister and I would be in Rippey for a visit, we always went to the cemetery with floral arrangements. If my memory serves me correctly (now that's a laugh), we would put out 20 some arrangements just in Rippey. We would also make the trip to other cemeteries in the area where ancestors are resting. Our children, Juleann, Bradley, and Cody were not too thrilled with these trips. Julene and I learned about "Decoration Day" from our Grandmother Nellie. I miss being able to put flowers out in person. I was so pleased to find a florist in Jefferson who will make a trip to Rippey with arrangements. That's Iowa for you.

Returning Home
By Becky Tiffany Zimmerman

Always something I have wanted to say, but it was a grand day when my mother returned to Rippey, even though it was to the cemetery. She loved Rippey.

Notes

Author Biographies

Clark Bardole: *Deceased 1994 at age 83.*

Esther Bardole: *Deceased 2002 at age 92.*

Julene Ann Rittgers Boza
Born in Rippey during a blizzard, February 10, 1939, to Wesley Rittgers and Lois Mae Humphrey Rittgers. Lived on Rittgers farm two miles south of Rippey. Kindergarten, the future Class of 1957; the last graduating class to walk across the small stage in the old gym of the school building where Wesley graduated in 1933.

Jean Darling Borgeson
Junior College study to become a lower elementary teacher. Moved to farm near Rippey in 1963 after marrying Ralph Borgeson. One daughter and three sons.

I joined the church choir the second Sunday after I was married, and soon became a Sunday School teacher and Junior Choir director. I enjoyed Eastern Star and Rebekah Lodges. Church, community, and school volunteer jobs helped me "sort out" Rippey families. Interest in my family tree expanded into a hobby that included many of my friends' family trees. I've always been grateful to be a Rippey Import!! I love the stories of the natives!

David Chase
Raised in Rippey (1947-1966) Graduated from East Greene (1966), from University of Northern Iowa (1970). Married Barbara in 1971. Graduated from University of Iowa Law School (1973). Practiced law in Atlantic, Iowa, (1973-2016). Now retired; avid tandem bicyclists, golfers and travelers. Currently reside in Atlantic, IA, and Keystone, CO.

Cindy Anderson Cole

Daughter of Walt and Nadine Anderson. Lived my entire life in Rippey. Graduated from East Greene 1972. Wayne State College degree in education 1976. Moved to Omaha 1976, married Ron Cole 1978. He is a retired Omaha Police Sergeant, and currently a school resource officer with Millard school district. I owned a private preschool for 26 years, retired, and now work as a part-time senior companion. Two daughters, 1 son, 3 grandchildren. I enjoy crafting, spending time with friends and family. Recently have reconnected with several high school friends and enjoy catching up on Rippey memories.

Duane Coon

Grew up on a farm NW of Rippey (1956 - 1975). I attended East Greene Schools, then on to Iowa State for a degree in Construction Engineering. My career began in Muscatine, IA, followed by Chicago, IL, and finally Rogers, AR. I retired in mid-2019 and will soon be building a new home for my wife and I just outside of Dubuque, IA.

Roger L. Crumley MD (RHS class of 1960)

I attended Simpson College, with John Bardole, Lynn Wilson, and Don Drake. Then U Iowa Med School (John Bardole a classmate), internship, then a year in VietNam '69-70 attached to Marines. Then 4 years ENT residency in Iowa City, 12 years at UC San Francisco, then U.C. Irvine after that. Married with 2 daughters. Proud of my Rippey Roots!

Gina ZANOTTI Dale

Relationship to Rippey: My grandfather, Andrew ZANOTTI, a resident beginning in 1930, my father Artage ZANOTTI, who was 6 years old in 1930 and later a graduate of Rippey High School, and my uncle, Lester ZANOTTI, who was born in 1936 and also a graduate of Rippey High School. Raised in Charles City, graduate U of

Iowa, resided in San Diego entire adult life. Enjoy my dad (95) and mom, uncle and aunt in SD winter months. Retired from automotive, and prior public relations company. Married, 3 stepkids, 7 grandchildren, avid sports fan, travel. Blessed.

Pat Daugherty
Grew up in Cumberland, IA; attended Simpson College and came to Rippey in 1958 to teach science and to coach. Went on to various administrative positions in other high schools and community colleges, ultimately becoming a coach and scout for the Colorado Rockies and the Montreal Expos. With wife JoAnne reside in Centennial, CO.

Clark Fessler
Grew up on a farm east of Rippey, with sister and brother. Graduated from East Greene in 1976. Farmed and had electrical and carpenter business in Rippey area following graduation. Moved to Perry, IA, and in 1987 started the beginnings of TC&B. In 1999 began import manufacturing while continuing to farm until 2009. President and CEO of TC&B located in Perry and Ho Chi Minh, Vietnam. Manufacturing Textile products. Reside with wife Lisa on banks of Beaver Creek near Berkley.

Jerald Fessler: *Deceased 2013 at age 78.*

Jim Fouch
Born in Jefferson, lived in Rippey from 1945 – 1967. Went to Rippey schools until senior year and graduated from East Greene HS in 1963. Went to the University of Denver and Illinois College of Optometry. I have 3 children, 3 step-children, 12 grandchildren and 1 great-grand daughter. I lived in Idaho for 50 years where I practiced Optometry for 45 years and now live in Meridian, Idaho, with my wife June and dog Ollie.

Fred Grow

Grew up on farm east of Rippey, 1946-1966; graduated from EGHS (1964). National Guard; AIB business school; married Jacquie Fagen 1966; moved to Boone and worked at Ecksteins Jewelry for 18 yrs. before purchasing the business, retiring in 2016; enjoy square dance calling and dancing and 4 grandchildren's activities.

Dale Hanaman

Married to Nancy Jean Bardole Hanaman. We were married at the Rippey Church June 8, 1968, visited every year, retired and moved to Nancy's family home July 1, 2007. I was a United Methodist pastor in Wisconsin for 39 years before retiring. I enjoy gardening, mowing, quilting, reading, and spending time with two children and spouses along with 5 grandchildren.

Nancy Bardole Hanaman

I grew up on a farm outside of Rippey with my parents, Clark and Esther Bardole and siblings, Sharon and John. I attended Rippey Schools until 1962 and graduated from East Greene in 1964. My husband, Dale, and I have lived in my childhood home since 2007.

Mary Ann Bardole Hick

I grew up on a farm west of Rippey. My parents were Paul and Mary Bardole. I was the baby of the family, with 4 older brothers and yes I was the only girl.

After graduating from high school, I went to Grand View College in Des Moines and got my Bachelor of Science in Nursing in 1980. I married my high school sweetheart, Kevin Hick, and we returned to Rippey where Kevin farmed with my dad and brother a few years and I worked at Greene County hospital. We have 2 children, Haven and Elizabeth, who also graduated from East Greene. I currently work at Mercy Hospital where I have worked in labor and delivery for 33 years. We enjoy being a part of the Rippey church and community all our lives.

Robert Huber
Lived on farms 3 1/2 miles from Rippey from 1950 until 1969. Received my college education at UNI. I began as a teacher at Charles City and eventually became a school counselor at Exira, South Tama, and Cedar Falls. My wife and I currently reside in Cedar Falls. We enjoy our two daughters, their husbands, and our two grandsons. My favorite stories are the true ones.

Carol Norgren John
Grew up south of Rippey. Went to Rippey Consolidated School through the 9th grade, then on to East Greene, graduated in 1965. Went off to UNI. Met and married David John, who grew up in Osceola, but who has family roots in Greene County dating back to 1856. Worked 33 years as a school librarian, the last 23 years in the Jefferson and Jefferson-Scranton school district. Over the years we have enjoyed traveling, mostly camping, throughout the U.S and a few other places. Now retired, we enjoy our acreage southwest of Jefferson, watching birds, riding our bikes, working on various projects, etc.

Jim F. Johnson, grandson of Franklin Johnson
While our family still owns the farm surrounding Old Rippey, I grew up in Atlantic, Iowa, and have now lived in Indiana for more than 20 years. I'm the Associate Director of the Student Involvement and Leadership Center at Indiana University in Bloomington.

Peter Johnson
Grew up in a family of eight in Grayling, MI. Worked for oil companies and it was my job that brought me to Iowa. Arrival eventually led me to my wife, the former Kate Brubaker. We were married and moved to Rippey in 1975.

Became a volunteer fire fighter for the Rippey Community at that time. Voluntarily trained to become an emergency medical responder, and currently serve as the Chief of the Rippey Fire Department.

Ellen Johnston
Ellen Johnston was born and raised in Rippey. She attended East Greene and graduated in 2000. Today, she lives and teaches overseas. Like the world, she is waiting to travel again.

Phyllis McElheney Lepke
Grew up on a farm south of Rippey (1947-1965). Earned three degrees from Iowa State and spent my professional career as an ISU faculty member, alumni administrator and fund-raising executive. Husband Larry and I enjoy travel anywhere and time spent with our son, Matthew. We have lived on an acreage near Story City, IA, for over 40 years, and now winter in Arizona.

Matthew Lepke
Visited my grandparents, Jack and Jean McElheney, on their farm south of Rippey, often from 1978 to their passings in 2006 and 2010, respectively. I enjoy baseball, hockey, the Iowa Hawkeyes, as well as exploring places through travel and photography.

Mary Fry Liebich
I grew up in Rippey. Attended Simpson (BA), the University of Iowa (MA) and University of Southern California (PhD). Taught at University of Wyoming, USC, Iowa State, Perry High and Jr High and Des Moines Area Community College. Married Rick Liebich and raised Richard. Have had horses since third grade. Rippey is home.

Sharon Bardole McBlain

I grew up on a farm near Rippey and graduated from Rippey High School in 1961 and have returned often ever since. I graduated from Simpson and married Phil in 1965. We started our antiquarian book business in Des Moines in 1971 and moved to Connecticut in 1983 with our teenage daughter, Kristina. My time is spent with books, Phil, friends, granddaughters and their parents, and volunteering with inner-city children.

Patricia Grow McPherson

I grew up south of Rippey on a farm started by my grandfather and grandmother Lawrence and Esther Grow. I have many memories growing up on the farm, celebrating life with family, the Rippey Methodist Church, and music and musicals at East Greene High School. I graduated from East Greene in 1971 and went on to get my BSN from Graceland College and later my Master's in HCA. I married Steve McPherson (teacher/elementary principal) from Jefferson and we had 2 daughters, Margie and Kristen. Most of my career was Nursing Administration ending at UnityPoint Hospital in Cedar Rapids. We love Iowa and have traveled some in Europe but prefer exploring the United States and our National Parks. Our biggest joys are our grandsons, Barrett and Colt. Happy Anniversary, Rippey!

Steve Nail

I grew up living in Rippey and attended the Rippey and East Greene Schools, graduating with the East Greene Class of 1969. After two years of Junior College, I entered the grain co-op business in Iowa. Since 1971, I have worked as a Co-op Assistant Manager or General Manager and am currently employed by Versova, one of the country's largest egg producers, as Director of Grain Merchandising.

Marna Rittgers Parker

I was born to Wesley and Lois Mae Rittgers in 1945 and spent my formative years in Rippey. I graduated from East Greene in 1964, and eventually made my way to Texas, where I currently reside. Even though I live in Texas, my heart is still in my hometown, Rippey.

Steven Pearson, grandson of Dale and Nancy Bardole Hanaman

A freshman at the University of Wisconsin-Superior with a history major and a coaching minor. He plans to teach and coach high school track. He was part of the soccer and track teams at Superior Senior High School.

John Rains

Moved to Rippey, 1959. Graduated East Greene 1964. Married 1969. Visited Mom and Dad (Roy and Evelyn Rains) until their deaths in May 1985 (Mom) and January 1998 (Dad). After college, worked 14 years for Massey Ferguson Farm Machinery Corporation, then 23 ½ years on Active Duty with the Army National Guard in the Recruiting and Retention Command, achieving rank of Sergeant Major. Hobby is Massey-Harris antique tractors and staying in touch with friends. Two sons and daughters-in-law, three grandsons. Live in Urbandale, IA.

Myron Rinker

Moved to Rippey from Boone and began working at the First National Bank in December of 1961. With wife, Maralynn, had two children, Marilee Rinker White and Marke Rinker. Have been an active member of the Rippey community as part of the Lions Club, Rippey United Methodist Church and the Rippey Commercial Club. Retired from working with the First National Bank and later Peoples Bank after 38 years in 1999.

Toni Averill Roberts

I grew up in Jefferson, Iowa, and was married to Phillip Roberts and moved to Rippey in 1964. We have four children, 13 grandchildren, and 16 great grandchildren. I was born to be a farmwife, as most of the time I enjoyed helping during the lambing season, as well as helping with field work. I was Rippey's Madam Librarian from 2005-2013.

Mike Scharingson

I grew up south of Rippey. East Greene 1969. ISU 1975. USAF 1971-1973. Iowa Air National Guard 1973-1978. 1975 Farming; 1992-2012 US Postal Service. DeAnn and I live north of Rippey. Daughters Jodi and Erin, 2 sons-in-law, 4 granddaughters. Hobbies: Family, ISU sports, reading, traveling.

Carol Thompson Sieck

I am a Rippey farm girl who attended Rippey School 1955-1963 and then East Greene from 1963 until I graduated in 1968. After college Allan and I returned to our family farm operation. In 1989 I went to work for the US Postal Service, retiring in 2012. We still live in our farm home SW of Rippey, where we raised our children, Jon, Josh, and Julianna.

CaroleAnne Souder Vannoy

I grew up on the Souder Family Farm south of Rippey from 1964 until 1982. I'm not sure at all how a country girl like myself ended up living in the city, but I followed in my grandmother's pathway and am teaching Iowa History for a Homeschool Co-Op in Urbandale, IA.

Mary Lee Dorris Weaver

Mary grew up on a farm northeast of Rippey and attended school in Rippey, graduating from East Greene in 1963.

She attended Nursing School at Iowa Methodist School of Nursing and went on to complete a B.S.N. from Grand View College in Des Moines, and M.S.N., from the University of Minnesota. She worked in public health nursing and at her retirement was the Director of Public Health Nursing for the State of Iowa.

She married Gary Weaver of Dana, and they had two children, David and Theresa. Their children married and she has three grandchildren. She and her husband are farmers and are engaged in farming with their son.

Lynn Wilson

Raised in Rippey, graduated 1959. B.A. Simpson College, M.A. University of Missouri. Eight years in advertising agency and direct mail business. 30 years with 3M in St. Paul. Married to Barb. Two sons and four grandsons. Traveled all states and internationally. Golf, fishing, boating, metal detecting. Live in Stillwater, MN.

Kathy Lansman Young

We moved to the Squirrel Hollow area when I was 6 in 1955. I was in Miss Wilson's 1st grade class. I was in the last 8th grade graduating class at Rippey and graduated from East Greene in '66. I worked for the State of Iowa Judicial Dept. for 28 years. I retired and moved to Denver, CO.

Linda Young

I was born in 1951 on the farm southeast of Rippey that my dad's grandparents bought in 1882, and later moved to the farm southwest of town my mom's grandparents bought in 1866. After graduating from East Greene in 1970, I studied journalism at University of Iowa, then worked for 35 years at newspapers in Davenport and Chicago, but I am most proud of being a fourth generation farm owner. I live in Brookfield, IL, but my heart will always be with the Rippey community where four generations of ancestors lie buried.

Les Zanotti

Rippey 1936-1954. Both parents buried there! Went to University of Iowa on a baseball scholarship and graduated in 1958. After two years in Army, bought an Executive Search franchise in Omaha and had 34 successful years. My wife, CeAnn, of 57 years and I have traveled to 26 different countries. We have a beautiful daughter, a great son-in-law, and 3 perfect grandchildren.

Becky Tiffany Zimmerman

Yes, I spent all my life in Rippey graduating in 1967. We had horses until my parents divorced and then things changed. Rode my bike all over to Dawson and Berkley. Had a paper route several summers. It was always an adventure going in the tank truck with GPA Murray and gathering eggs at the Jenkins farm. I spent much time on the farm with Jim and Marj Benshoof but my best memories are still at home. Rippey Rocks.

Acknowledgments

Thank you to the 42 authors of remembrances, stories, family and town histories, serious and funny reflections, who participated in writing this book.

The nearly 60 entries were coordinated by Phyllis McElheney Lepke, and our book was designed and printed by Raspberry Ridge Publishing, Janice Harbaugh, Editor, of Jefferson, Iowa.

Sarah Killgore serves as our webmaster and has posted "I Remember Rippey" items online every week for more than a year. Special thanks to you, Sarah.

Friends of Rippey
Summer 2020

Available Now!

AUTHENTIC BRAND

PLATES
$10.00 Each
$7.00 S&H
(prefer pickup)

HATS
$10.00 Each
$5.00 S&H

SHIRTS
$10.00 Each
$5.00 S&H

Checks can be sent to:
Friends of Rippey
P.O. Box 52
Rippey, IA

For more information, call: 515-360-8046

Manufactured by TC and B Corporate Wearables (Clark Fessler's company)

Friends of Rippey

BUY A BRICK PROGRAM

We are raising money to help pay for a patio area in front of the Rippey School
Memorial. The bricks will be placed in front of the memorial, facing the circle drive.
The cost is $50.00 per brick.

- -

Yes, we'd like to reserve a permanent brick. Please engrave our brick as follows:

ANY SYMBOL IS CONSIDERED ONE SPACE (PERIOD, COMMA, DASH, HYPEN)
ALL TEXT IS CENTERED UNLESS OTHERWISE NOTED

EXAMPLE

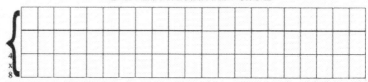

PLEASE RETURN THIS FORM AND YOUR CHECK PAYABLE TO: **Friends of Rippey**
PO Box 52
Rippey, IA 50235

Name: _____ Phone: (_____) _____
Address: _____
City: _____ State: _____ Zip: _____
Email Address: _____ Amount Paid: _____

If you have any questions, please call Mary Weaver at 515-360-8046.

Memorial Donations

for the Rippey Sesquicentennial
Made by individuals and families to honor their
deceased loved ones

Kathy Jensen for Daniel Peters
John Rains for Roy and Evelyn Rains
Robert Huber for Dennis Nail
John Lint for Judy Lint
Betty Griffith for Carson Griffith
John and Janis Turpin for Carl and Wanda King
    and Marcia King Brink
Nation Family for Jack Nation
               for Virgene Nation
Kyle Mower for Ben Vannatta
Renee L. Rains for Roy and Evelyn Rains,
    and Jerry Rains
Frances Teagarden for Jack Teagarden
Steve Nail for Dick and Barb Nail,
    Theresa Nail Hague, Dennis Nail
Harve and Joyce Rice for Barney Rice

Made in the USA
Middletown, DE
19 September 2020